EX LIBRIS

Jo Ann & John Fisher

SELECTED LETTERS

of

EDWIN ARLINGTON ROBINSON

THE MACMILLAN COMPANY
NEW YORK · BOSTON · CHICAGO
DALLAS · ATLANTA · SAN FRANCISCO

MACMILLAN AND CO., LIMITED
LONDON · BOMBAY · CALCUTTA
MADRAS · MELBOURNE

THE MACMILLAN COMPANY
OF CANADA, LIMITED
TORONTO

Photograph by Pirie MacDonald

SELECTED LETTERS

OF

Edwin Arlington Robinson

1940

THE MACMILLAN COMPANY

NEW YORK

PRINTED IN THE UNITED STATES OF AMERICA
AMERICAN BOOK—STRATFORD PRESS, INC., NEW YORK

. . . the race where that immortal garland is to be run for, not without dust and heat.

MILTON, "Areopagitica"

INTRODUCTION

"I DON'T care for X's letters," Robinson once said of a correspondent. "They read as though he had written them for posterity."

There is a world of poetry and there is a world of letter-writing and hardly the two shall meet. Writers in either field had best address themselves to their appointed hearers, the poet to the universe, the letter-writer to one person chosen out of earth's hurrying multitudes. It should become clear on reading the letters assembled in this volume that the writer of them had no double purpose. In his letter-writing as in his life he kept his eye single.

But what if posterity, in spite of him, should turn from his poetry to his letters in search of his human quality? Such natural curiosity will not go unrewarded. Indeed posterity, if it pleases, will know far more about him than was known during his lifetime, when brief impression and popular report labeled him a shy New Englander whose writing outsoared his speech as the lark the snail. This in fact was true, part of the time. But if he was a poet, first of all, he was also emphatically a human being, and not all his reticence can keep his letters from revealing the warmth, genuineness and variety of his human relationships.

The good fortune of being lawful heir to previous generations, which each age holds in turn, must be paid for by certain privations, as, for example, our never having seen Blake or heard Coleridge. But there are always compensations, and our successors will not be without theirs. True, they will never see Robinson sitting in a room full of chatterers, with eyes excessively bright and lips completely silent, pressing his long fingers to his forehead, or hear him when he was in the rare vein, with one or two intimates, talking very well indeed after all.

But they will be able to see, in his letters, the ease, intimacy and utterly natural playfulness with which he expressed himself when inhibitions were removed. They can find the man who actually made a cult of friendship and who, as far as his friends were concerned, needed the solacing exchange of letters more, perhaps, than if he had more freely sustained the relationship with spoken words.

The contrast between the fountains pressing up in his earliest letters to his boyhood friend, Arthur Gledhill, and the more restrained flow of his later expression should not surprise those who knew him only in his later years. He wrote to Gledhill at an age when the need to be understood is an unendurable urge. There were few in the young poet's countryside to whom he could make the immensely important confession, ". . . writing has been my dream since I was old enough to lay plans for an air castle." Few indeed to whom he could speak of the lions that lay in wait for him on his fateful pilgrimage: ". . . if I make a failure of it and the chances are ten to one that I shall, my life will be a disappointment and a failure."

With Gardiner and Harvard behind him and with Fame who could say how far ahead, the early letters from New York show a no less urgent need of intimate human understanding—and something besides. He has found his idiom as a writer. He is deepening the sureties which were to last his lifetime. The letters to Miss Peabody and to Mr. Mason are the symptoms, to regard them clinically, of that mountain fever which forever lurks in the foothills of Parnassus. And he was impelled, as every young artist is impelled, to compare his chart with those of others who, he felt, were also in their own ways fever-stricken. This latter need it was but natural that he should shortly outgrow. But the need for mere human relationships did not diminish with the years, and so long as life lasted this apparently solitary figure clung closely to the living bulwarks of affection to which he had attached himself.

Though his friendships were divided impartially between men and women, though he was a man's man as much as a woman's, he felt, like most highly sensitive men, most at his ease in writing to women. In his letters to Mrs. Richards he disagrees, domineers, makes discreet love, digs up old sparkling gayeties and slyly contrives new ones, tossing up the bright fancies before her with the skill of the juggler performing for the madonna.

This acute consciousness of the person to whom he was writing accounts for the variety of his letters. Though he was at the very antipodes of being all things to all men, he wrote in a special language and of special matters to each correspondent. Furthermore, his sensitiveness led him to write well in proportion as his correspondent had liberated him from his deep native reserve and proven the ability to understand him. "I have many things to tell you but you cannot bear them now."

It is fortunate that for the present collection a goodly part, at least, of the letters of Robinson's early years has been made available. These were of course his most critical years. While it is a matter of regret that certain important groups of letters are still unshared by their recipients or present owners, it may be that such sections of his correspondence could, after all, add no more poignant emphasis to the gropings of his adolescence, the ardors of his maturity. Nor could any letters throw into sharper relief the fact that, youth once passed, the many and prolonged difficulties that beset him were of his exterior life only. His inner course by this time held true to the light of his particular North Star.

For the rest, the letters chosen show a life exceptional in its apparent detachment. They show a life-long concentration upon the one thing that mattered and that he never, even for a moment, lost sight of; and they tell of his firm, unbroken friendships. In Robinson's case this is pretty much the whole story and it is a story well worth telling.

If there is one piece of advice which those who knew him well might offer to inquiring after-comers it would be not to look in his letters for what isn't there, not to expect to find his secret, the springs of his mystery. It is true that in the letters to Gledhill, when he was very young, he lets through certain gleams, mostly oblique, from the inmost places. But soon the boyish confessions end. We read no more in that book. With this key he did not unlock his heart. But for that matter, neither did he in his poetry. He was not that kind of poet. And he was not that kind of letter-writer.

In bringing together the letters included in this volume, chosen from the large body of correspondence made available, the intent has been to present Robinson the man. Although material of a biographical nature is not primarily a part of the book's design, some has inevitably found its way into the text and will, it is hoped, further enrich the reader's conception of the poet.

Special thanks should be expressed to Hermann Hagedorn, Lewis M. Isaacs, and Louis V. Ledoux, who have collaborated with the writer in the preparation of this volume. Owing to his absence in Europe, Percy MacKaye, one of the five originally chosen, has been unable to accept a share in the work.

Acknowledgement is due to all who have placed letters at the disposal of the editors.

RIDGELY TORRENCE

New York, September, 1939

BIOGRAPHICAL NOTE

EDWIN ARLINGTON ROBINSON *was born at Head Tide, Maine, December 22, 1869, the third son of Edward and Mary Elizabeth (Palmer) Robinson. In the following year the family moved to Gardiner, Maine, where the poet later attended the public schools, graduating from High School in 1889. He spent the years 1891 to 1893 at Harvard. In 1896 he privately published his first collection of poems,* The Torrent and the Night Before. *A second volume,* The Children of the Night, *was published in 1897. In 1900 he moved to New York City. In 1902 his volume* Captain Craig and Other Poems *appeared. In 1905 President Theodore Roosevelt, through admiration of his poetry, gave him a position in the New York Custom House and shortly afterward reviewed* The Children of the Night *in* The Outlook. *In 1909 Robinson resigned from the Customs service and in 1910 published* The Town Down the River. *In 1911 he went to the MacDowell Colony at Peterborough, New Hampshire, which continued to be his summer residence for the remainder of his life. He spent the spring of 1923 in England. In 1927, with* Tristram, *one of three of his long poems on Arthurian themes, he achieved his first popular success.*

Among his more than twenty volumes of poetry are The Man Against the Sky, *1916;* Merlin, *1917;* The Three Taverns, *1920;* Avon's Harvest, *1921;* The Man Who Died Twice, *1924;* Dionysus in Doubt, *1925;* Sonnets, *1928;* Cavender's House, *1929;* The Glory of the Nightingales, *1930;* Matthias at the Door, *1931;* Nicodemus, *1932;* Amaranth, *1934;* King Jasper, *1935. He also published two prose plays:* Van Zorn, *1915, and* The Porcupine, *1916.*

He died at the New York Hospital, April 5, 1935.

I
THE START
(Aetat. 20–29)

TO ARTHUR R. GLEDHILL

Gardiner, Apr. 17, 1890

LAST NIGHT I copied off "Palaemon" and have herewith enclosed the same.[1] You will find it rather loose for an attempt at poetical translation and you may have some trouble in deciphering it. But as you have read the original and are acquainted with the subject I guess you can follow the lines. Yesterday I finished a translation (blank verse) of the "Galley Race", Book V, 104-285. I have also made one of the "Last Combat", Book XII, 788-952 and "The Shield of Aeneas", Book VIII, 597-731. Great sport but devilish hard work. In the "Galley Race" I worked two days on two lines—that is to say, it was two days before I decided. This was the place:

—Illa Noto citius volucrique sagitta
Ad terram fugit et portu se condidit alto. 242-243

"Swift as the wind, in arrowy flight she speeds
And rides triumphant in the land-locked port."

Don't be too harsh in your criticism but write and tell me what you think of it. You will notice the body of the thing to be in pentameters while the singing match is in Alexandrine couplets—as I wished to retain the appearance of the original as much as possible. Box all right. Thanks.

If it is a possible thing I will come up your way some time this spring. I should like to have a smoke with you and see the Diva.[2]

3

TO ARTHUR R. GLEDHILL

Gardiner, July 24, 1890

. . . Dean is weighing ice down at Smithtown, for the Knickerbockers, and consequently I am left here alone with Mother to take care of the "farm" and look after my father. He is no better, and taking things all around my life is rather a dull one, though of course I cannot complain. But still it make one uneasy to realize that he is sliding off into the majority and as far as a regular occupation is concerned is nothing but a drone, with no particular opening for the future. I tell you what it is, Art, sometimes a week or ten days goes by without my seeing one of the boys or girls (I believe I never saw much of *them,* anyway) unless I happen to run across them down street in the afternoon for a minute or two. I never was much of a light in company, but it hardly suits me to become a genuine eremite. Perhaps if I had something like your "anchor" to take up my thoughts, life would seem different but such a state of affairs is hardly probable, and besides, Hippolytus never meddled with females. . . .

Keep on with your pedagogic work and go through college if you can; and sometimes when you are strolling around the campus after twilight, alone . . . you may think of the fellow down east who never seemed to amount to much in school (or anywhere else) but who was proud to believe that he was not altogether a nincompoop. He never had a great many friends, this fellow, but those he did have he has never forgotten, and never will. He could forget a petty insult or injury very easily but somehow or other he never could forget a favor, however small. Living by himself as he does with a father who can hardly walk a step without his help it is not so strange that he should occasionally have an attack of something bordering on the blues. You know nothing about it, and I hope you never will. . . .

If one of our old set should drop out there would be something gone from our own lives. Longfellow says,

"*Something is gone from nature since they died*
And summer is not summer, nor can be."

That would be the case; but I hope there is no reason for such thoughts. . . .

TO ARTHUR R. GLEDHILL

Gardiner, Aug. 14, 1890

. . . You say that the future stretches before you to be seized with earnest hands, etc. Seize it, by all means, but don't regret that you were enabled to enjoy two years as you never will again. No, Art, in all probability you never will again browse over Cooper's *Virgil* or climb into the laboratory to smoke the fragrant academic pipe; you will never roost upon the belfry rafters and chew the contemplative weed that you and I have now forsaken; you will never again balance yourself to open that well-remembered scuttle to let the fumes escape and float away into the winter air, and you will hear no more the melted snow and ice dropping upon the tin roof over your head.

It is possible, but hardly probable that we, the old "three", together with Doc, will take another "half-day off", and stretch ourselves beneath the shadows of the "Pines" (you will hear the wind soughing through them yet, sometime when you are alone in after years) as we did in the fall of '87. Yes, it is all over. It will be many years before I shall drift across the common and find you stretched upon the seat where the four walks meet near the G. H. S., a little after one o'clock and the *"check"* will be produced as in days of yore. Remember from Virgil:

> *"Forsan et haec olim meminisse juvabit,"*

and don't for God's sake labor under the delusion that those days were wasted. This world is at best a diabolically practical place and if you are able to draw a little poetry somewhere out of the past—do it. I know how you feel now with your "large and loyal love", but I tell you what it is, old man, the time will come when you will realize that life was something before you came to Spencer. Some dark night you will lie awake and listen to the rain falling upon the roof; your thoughts will travel down to Maine, and your head will be full of belfries, laboratories, *"arma virumque cano"*, Miss Austen, Stuart, Moore, Sawyer, and you may gaze into phantom clouds of smoke and meet the face of

ROBINSON

TO ARTHUR R. GLEDHILL

Gardiner, Sept. 27, 1890

. . . No, Art, I have entirely given up all ideas of going to college; my school education was completed when I left the friendly doors of the G. H. S. If I had not made the mistake that I did in supposing that it would be impossible for me to take a college course on account of "home rule", things would have probably turned out in a different manner. Father always talked down colleges and claimed they did men no good; and consequently when I entered the high school I never gave the thing a thought. It was not until I entered the first class that I began to consider the question seriously and I am afraid the fact is that I had not the *sand* to turn back the leaves that I had so carelessly scanned, and prepare myself. If this is the case, of course a college course would have been a failure if I had planned for it from the first. Last week I worked with Danforth, the civil engineer, and by that means got a month's work on the River Survey which will turn me about fifty dollars. I begin next Monday. It is a diabolical business, to my taste, but I can hardly afford to let such chances slip through my fingers. . . .

TO ARTHUR R. GLEDHILL

Harvard University, Cambridge
Nov. 14, 1891

. . . I feel as if I had always been here, and as if I should always like to stay here. If there is any class of people in the world that I envy, they are the Freshmen, who have four years of Harvard life before them instead of eight months. However, I am not growling, but consider myself fortunate as it is. I "sprung" a ballade on the *Advocate* a while ago. Much to my surprise, it was accepted. The *Ad.* prints some of the best amateur fiction that I have ever seen. Will send you a copy if I can think of it. Perhaps you see it, though, in the office of your own paper. That is the great difference between a small college and a large one. You can get acquainted, if you wish to, with about every fellow at the place, while I am doing well to be on familiar terms with two or three. That is enough for me, though; I never cared for a "host of friends"—I don't believe in them. . . .

This afternoon (Saturday) I am going into town to see Whitney and take a turn into the theater in the evening. Wish you were here to go with us. Went last Sat. evening to see Modjeska in *Macbeth* and was completely disappointed. She was well enough, but what little voice her trembling hus-

band had was lost in his moustache. Taken all around it was
a big fizzle. But the house was crowded, myself a gallery
god. Whitney suffered through the whole thing and I felt
rather guilty in persuading him to go with me. . . .

TO ARTHUR R. GLEDHILL

1716 Cambridge St., Cambridge
Dec. 10, '92
. . . I am fairly crowded with work just at present. Have
German five times a week and beside my regular written
work an eight thousand word thesis to write on the British
Periodical Essayists, which is to be handed in right after
New Year's. I expect to go home the 23rd, but may stop over
one day for the Symphony concert. I am getting to be a
fiend for that kind of a thing though my experience is limited. Yesterday afternoon I went to hear Damrosch's orchestra at the Tremont Theatre. They played Beethoven's Third
Symphony, Grieg's "Aus Holberg's Zeit" (the best thing I
ever heard) and a selection from "Tannhäuser". Symphonies
& grand operas are a perfect revelation to me and I am curs-
ing myself for letting so many go by last year. . . .

TO ARTHUR R. GLEDHILL

1716 Cambridge St.
May 23, '93
. . . This "job" question is beginning to interest me to an
extent that it never did before. Most of the people who have
them seem to be better off than those who do not, but most
of the people are not so hopelessly fettered by their individual tastes as I am. I do not wish to teach school or work

with tools or much of anything else that brings money to a man. And yet I do not consider myself altogether lazy. I feel that things are coming out all right some time but the action is slow. This is my last week at Harvard—excepting the examinations. The idea of leaving seems a little strange, but I doubt if I should care to come another year under the circumstances. I am getting to be an old man and must do something to bring in the ducats instead of throwing them out all the time. . . .

TO ARTHUR R. GLEDHILL

Gardiner, Oct. 28, '93

. . . You and Ed are making me feel old, with your marrying and looking out for yourself—excuse me—yourselves. I do not see any immediate chance of my amounting to anything though I have by no means given the thing up. This itch for authorship is worse than the devil and about spoils a man for anything else. Perhaps I have never given you to understand that this is what ails me, but such is the case. I will make a clean confession and say that writing has been my dream ever since I was old enough to lay a plan for an air castle. Now for the first time I seem to have something like a favorable opportunity and this winter I shall make a beginning. If I make a failure of it, and the chances are about ten to one that I shall, my life will be a disappointment and a failure. I do not know much about the ways of successful men and the thing called "business" was always a bugbear and a mystery to me. Business men are necessities I suppose, and all I ask of them is to keep themselves as such out of my way. If I had a little of your general intellect, and faculty of making yourself popular wherever you go, life would be a different thing for me. I have lived nearly twenty-four years, and am thankful chiefly that I haven't them to live over again. So you see my life hasn't been such a pleasant affair as some men's seem to be. Perhaps it is partly my own fault, but I hardly understand how it can be so to any great extent. Well, I will not growl on in this way. You are beginning the second period of your life now, and I hope that you are as happy as your letter indicates. I do not imagine that you are rich, but do not let that bother you. My money has all gone to the devil in a bad investment and I am as poor as need be. But that is all right. The loss of money is a small thing after all, compared with other things.

Sometimes I almost fancy I see you coming into the yard as you used to, with your hands in your trousers pockets. . . . Those were good days. I suppose they have pretty much disappeared from your thoughts by this time, but it is different with me. Some little incident that gave me pleasure five or six years ago will come back to me in all its foolish simplicity and cheer me up to an extent that seems incredible. Were I not so much a fool, perhaps it would be otherwise. But then about [all] I find here in Gardiner to interest me is what I conjure up from my own fancy and so perhaps I am not so much an ass as I am inclined to think sometimes, and I long to get back to Cambridge with a den of my own to do and think as I please in. Owing to many things of a domestic nature my life there was about one-fourth as pleasant as it would have been otherwise, but for all that I am thankful for the time I was able to spend there. It seems more like a dream now than anything else, but I can feel the change it has made in me. I am a better man with better ideals than I was before I went, but I am afraid they are not the ideals to help me in the active walk of life, whatever they may be. . . .

I will ask you to be generous enough not to give me up

altogether for a time at least. I may do something to make myself respectable and eventually earn enough to pay for what I eat and wear. I do not dare to look farther than that at present. . . . Do not judge my chances in literature by this letter, as it would be cruelty to me. I am inclined to be a little too colloquial in my correspondence—a fault which I shall ask you to overlook.

TO ARTHUR R. GLEDHILL

Gardiner, 20 August '95

. . . It makes me sick to look back upon the life that I have lived in the past, and almost so to look into the future, that is, sometimes. I have faith in myself—too much of it, I think, but I was sent into this world without the strength to stand up under my ambitions. I always came home "tuckered" when I was a kid with the rest of the boys and am afraid that it will always be the case. I have never been able to think of myself as more than 30 or 35 years old and I am not sure that I desire to be more than that. I have presentiments, and have always had them, but I am very glad to say that they are not all gloomy. One of them is that the fellows who know me best are not going to forget me and another is that I am going to do something before I get through. There is, I think, nothing morbid in my condition. My common sense just tells me that there is not enough of me, and never was, to last a great many years. This is no new thing with me and it does not scare me in the least. I am not suicidal, nor am I a vegetarian. I am not a pessimist, or anything of the sort. My optimism and chronic appreciation of a joke, if it be a good one, are what will save me. I have no conception of discouragement and am not altogether lazy. I shall never be a Prominent Citizen and I thank God for it, but I shall be something just as good perhaps and possibly a little more permanent. . . .

TO ARTHUR R. GLEDHILL

Gardiner, Oct. 28, 1896

. . . For some reason, letter writing comes hard to me nowadays and it is only once in four or five weeks that I feel in anything like the mood for it. My philosophy tells me not to give up to moods, but what the devil is a fellow going to do when he knows well enough that if he writes he is bound to make a dismal ass of himself? I can make the ink go today, but I won't swear to my good sense or to my syntax. In fact, I don't worry about either for I know you will excuse my shortcomings on the ground of human nature. Sometimes we talk sense, and sometimes we don't; and sometimes the last named accomplishment is the more attractive. This is why I have faith in myself.

I am going to have that book of poems ready in a few days and of course I shall send you an inscribed copy (That sounds good!). I couldn't succeed in persuading any publisher to take the stuff so I'm printing it on my own hook for an experiment—the Riverside Press is doing the job and they are doing it well. The typography will be above reproach but the genius of the contents may be open to some questioning. That is all right, however; I have got to the point now where criticism has no more effect on me than cheese—nor half so much. Cheese binds me up like the devil, while criticism binds me down to persistent "swelled head" and harder work. You won't find much in the book to interest you, but, considering you know the man who did it, you may like to look it over. You won't find much in the way of natural description. There is very little tinkling

water, and there is not a red-bellied robin in the whole collection. When it comes to "nightingales and roses" I am not
"in it" nor have I the smallest desire to be. I sing, in my
own particular manner, of heaven & hell and now and then
of natural things (supposing they exist) of a more prosy
connotation than those generally admitted into the domain
of metre. In short I write whatever I think is appropriate
to the subject and let tradition go to the deuce. This may
not be a safe plan, but there is no end of personal satisfaction in it. This book will probably mark the end of my
poetical career (that sounds good, too) for I am full to the
muzzle with prose ideas, which may or may not come to a
head. I don't know that it makes any particular difference
whether they do or not, as long as I have 'em. . . .

I have been slowly getting rid of materialism for the past
year or two, but I fear I haven't the stamina to be a Christian—accepting Christ as either human or divine. Selfishness
hangs to a man like a lobster and is the thing that keeps
humanity where it is, I know that, but at present I am pretty
much a human being, though I see a glimmer of the light
once in a while and then meditate on possibilities. You will
find my need, as far as I have one, in two or three of the
shorter poems. "The Night Before" is an attempt to be
absolutely impersonal which, of course, is an impossibility.

TO JOHN HAYS GARDINER

135 West 64th St., New York
2 January, 1898

I was very glad to hear from you but sorry to learn that
you were not feeling well. I trust you are yourself
again by this time, though I don't quite understand how
a man can be himself and still read themes. I could rake

the college yard, but I couldn't (for more than one reason) do the work that you English men are doing. I look on you as heroes, and feel sorry for myself that I can do so little for the young idea. The art of shooting is something I never learned—and so am disqualified to teach. Of course a man can teach a good deal that he doesn't know, but he can't teach English Composition without knowing at least the first principles of Rhetoric. Whatever accidental decency there may be in what I have done is a matter of instinct and hard work. Whether it is grammar or not I have no means of knowing; and as for solecisms, I'm afraid I've forgotten what they are.

I thank you for the enclosed clippings from the *Transcript*. If you know who wrote them kindly give my thanks to that person for his friendly interest & appreciation. There was "internal evidence" in the longer article to make me think you might not be wholly ignorant as to its origin. Please remember me to Mr. Wendell, Mr. Baker, Mr. Hayes and the rest of them.

For the present I prefer New York to Boston and should prefer London to New York. I have a queer feeling that I should like to camp for a week at the foot of the Great Pyramid. Nordau has a name for this but I don't remember it.

TO JOHN HAYS GARDINER

Gardiner, 2 November, 1898

I am very glad to learn that there seems to be some shadow of a chance for me in Cambridge, and I feel, naturally, that I ought not to be too independent in regard to the conditions. As I said before you went away, next October would suit me best; but of course I should be willing to go in the spring, or before then, if necessary. The book is nearly all written in the rough, but the real labor is still to come; and there is enough of it to occupy nearly all of my time for the next six months. If the matter cannot easily be put over until October, I should prefer to try about the middle of April or the first part of May, but I am quite ready to try it anytime rather than run any chance of losing it.—Yes, I think I can take a run to Cambridge sometime in the winter. As for a place to sleep—I am all right. By a judicious manipulation of friends, acquaintances, and relatives, I suppose I might stay in your neighborhood for a couple of months, if I chose to do so, without paying any hotel bills.

Donne

I find I have acquired a kind of artificial taste for your friend Donne but I shall never be able to share your enthusiasm. He is both dogmatic and ancient, like my stationery, and hardly to be considered as apart from his period —which is, to my mind, sufficient damnation for any writer —particularly a poet, who must be, if he is to be anything, an interpreter of life. Donne, looking at him from the larger point of view, doesn't seem to me to interpret much more than a sort of half-mystical sexual uneasiness and a rather uninteresting religious enthusiasm which seems to have been quite the thing in those days for a fellow who had raised the devil for thirty-five or forty years and so worked up an appetite for symbols. Very likely I am all wrong, as usual, but I can only tell you what I think.

Professor James' book is entertaining and full of good things; but his attitude toward Spencer makes me think of a dream my father once had. He dreamed he met a dog. The dog annoyed him, so he struck him with a stick. Then the dog doubled in size and my father struck him again with the same result. So the thing went on till the universe was pretty much all dog. When my father awoke, he was, or rather had been, half-way down the dog's throat.—I can't for the life of me understand how the professor can reconcile his distressingly clever discovery of "a metaphysical creed" and a "tea table elysium" on the Spencerian system with Spencer's own careful statements to the effect that there can be no such a thing as a moral science but as drawn from the tangible progress of events, and measured from the point of view of a postulated ideal. The professor seems to be shrieking for the recognition of something like this as if it were his own discovery of the nebular hypothesis. He doesn't seem to see that Spencer's philosophy includes his own, for what it is worth, and that his self-elected position as metaphysical funny man is almost pathetically unimpressive. Very likely I am wrong again, but I don't think so.— I do not refer at all to the chapter on Hegel.—Thanking you most sincerely for your friendly work on my account.

TO JOHN HAYS GARDINER

Gardiner, 14 November, 1898
I must hasten to correct your impression that I am coming to Boston "for a month or two". I was merely telling you what was possible when I referred to such a visit. The fact is, I am going to Winthrop in a week or so for a short stay and after that, for the winter. My trip to Cambridge will be wholly on account of the "job" and I shall probably make it very short—not from choice, but because I am now, for the first time in my life, beginning to realize that days and weeks have a kind of value.—Somehow I cannot bring myself to feel very sanguine in regard to getting this position, but I shall be just as much obliged to you whether I do or not. In the latter case I shall have to emigrate and "do" whatever relations I can find.

When it comes to Spencer's style, I am afraid I cannot

be quite so vehement in his defense. Still it is sincere (you will not admit this) and it intends to be dignified, while James's is forever prostituting itself to contemporary slang and slipshod affectations, by which he hopes, I suppose, to strike the popular chord and conceal its arrogance. This is pretty ungenerous criticism, but I cannot think for a minute that the man is unconscious of what he is doing. If he is not, there is certainly a smallness in him that I would not suspect, and a spiritual vulgarity not wholly unrelated to that of the Reverend Talmage.—My reading of the Bible, the Old Testament, has been much like my reading of the original text of Confucius. I must follow your example and make up for my past neglect. Remember me to Mason. [Postscript]

Mrs. Richards is reading Amiel's *Journal* and she is likely to read *Evelyn Innes*.

TO DANIEL GREGORY MASON

1716 Cambridge St.
19 June, 1899

I do not think I shall be able to see you tomorrow noon, but I shall be ready for the Pop in the evening. There is a particularly good programme and I hope you will not be off the hook—which is better than indisposed.—I stretched out yesterday and read *Walking*, but did not quite relish what seemed to me to be a sort of glorified Thoreau cowardice all through the thing. For God's sake, says the sage, let me get away into the wilderness where I shall not have a single human responsibility or the first symptoms of social discipline, let me be a pickerel or a skunk cabbage, anything that will not have to meet the realities of civilization. There is a wholesomeness about some people that is positively unhealthy, and I find it in this essay. Still I am ready for *Walden*. If I hear nothing from you I shall make my appearance at about six-thirty.

TO DANIEL GREGORY MASON

1716 Cambridge St.
14 July, 1899

I got your card this morning and am sorry to learn that you are not joyous in Dublin. If at the end of another week you find yourself still unreconciled to your ladder and haymow (I understand from Miss Peabody that you have something of the kind) I hope you will do the wise thing and come back to Boston, which is, after all, about as good a place as a man can find. You cannot afford to mortgage yourself too much this summer or to give in to the rather bottomless notion that you must go somewhere in order to rest. Of course private matters may stand in the way, but if they do not—if you are tolerably sure of finding quiet on English ground—I think I will ply you to do so. I appreciate, however, that there are many and peculiar difficulties attending the man who has a piano for a gripsack.— At any rate, don't become a "depression" to yourself. You can't become such to your friends—to those who know you —but you may raise the devil with your own spiritual self-respect—which is very bad for the cerebrospinal apparatus and a menace even to the vermiform appendix.

Do you know that I have wondered sometimes if Savage [1] was not often the victim of what the world has a way of calling an excellent situation? Very likely this is fancy, but those infernal photographs of him tell me things that it makes me sick to think of. The octopus of superficial self-respect as opposed to the other, which I grant may be

carried too far—he refuses for some reason to take hold
of me—is more than anything that Hugo or Jules Verne
ever dreamed of, and I cannot but feel half-afraid that
Savage lost himself in the black water with which this particular beast is said to bewilder his victim.

This is all very tragic, but I do not mean it to apply to
you except as a warning for the next two months. I have
a way of pounding my friends with clubs when I mean
merely to touch them with my overgrown right hand and
caution them not to lose all of their time in a semi-hysterical
attempt to improve it. I have come to the conclusion (almost) that it will be impossible for me to undertake any
kind of useful occupation during the coming years and I have
racked my brains to find a way to get through them for
myself. Now I think—largely through good luck—that I
have done it. I am in ridiculously good spirits just now,
sending the *Pauper* [2] along at a rate that makes him red in
the face, eating anything that comes along, drinking nothing
unpermitted by the laws of Cambridge, and feeling every
morning the joy of a liberated idiot for the thought that I
am no longer a "necessity" in University 5. The beauty
of it is that I look on the place with an almost pathetic
affection, the pathos, however, is without longing and without qualms. Come to Cambridge and see me or go to
Provincetown.

TO DANIEL GREGORY MASON

1716 Cambridge Street
27 August, 1899

. . . The principal thing I have to tell you is that I am
reading Emerson's *Conduct of Life* for the first time. I confess this with burning shame, but that is not enough. It

should be read by everybody before they look at so much as
the title page of the *Essays,* whatever chronology may have
to say. In the essay on "Power" he takes one over his
paternal knee and wallops one with a big New England
shingle for about three-quarters of a New England hour.
He really gets after one: "A day is a more magnificent cloth
than any muslin, the mechanism that makes it is infinitely
cunninger, and you shall not cancel the sleezy, fraudulent,
rotten hours you have slipped into the piece; nor fear that
any honest thread, on straighter steel or more inflexible shaft
will not testify in the web." This is not exactly original, but
coming as it does at the end of the whole thing it does admirable work.—If you will read this book carefully you
will get changed ideas of Emerson's humanity and humor.
I am ready to confess, however, that the human note has a
faint suggestion of falsetto here and there, but, on the
other hand, may not that suggestion be the product of my
own diabolical system rather than of Emerson's idealism?—
Do not think from this that I am throwing away all of my
time, for I am not. My interesting and impoverished poor
man [1]—who is something of a scholar but not "me", as I
fancy you have suspected—has now consumed over a thousand lines of more or less grammatical English, but not just
the kind that would pull an A in English 12. I'm against
subtility and adroitness for the most part, I am afraid,
though I can be as subtle as the devil on particular occasions. . . .

TO DANIEL GREGORY MASON

1716 Cambridge St.
7 September, 1899
. . . I saw Miss Peabody last evening and found her
divinely wound up. She talked a blue streak, as the Philis-

tines would say (it is lucky for me that I am not a Philistine) and thereby made it very comfortable for me. All I had to do was to keep her going with an occasional turn to keep the spring tight. I find good news in Schopenhauer and a good deal of obvious indignation. The *cum grano salis* method, which he takes for granted, must never be discarded. It is inconceivable that a man of such wonderful insight could get so pitiably askew on occasions. Mr. Vaughan [1] does not give me any new thrills, but his ghost has my staunch gratitude for the Preface, which is enough to immortalize three men. He did not intend it to be funny, but, then, things are not always what we intend them to be, a truth, which needs an almighty medium somewhere. Here is a poem by Kipling.[2] You must know it. There is music enough as a poem but I don't know about it as a song. It will be worth reading again anyhow. I find Santayana's book unexpectedly wooden. He has enough to say, and he says it well; but somehow it seems like something written by a highly sophisticated corpse. If Santayana ever cuts himself in your presence try to get some of his blood.

TO DANIEL GREGORY MASON

Boston, Sept. 12, 1899

After reading your letter in the South Station I walked out, with all possible casualness and unconsciousness, and found myself in a strange land. It must have been somewhere in Boston but it was almost anywhere except Summer Street. Some day next week I am going down there again and see how I did it. I am always interested when I get lost in Boston, and that is undoubtedly one of the reasons why my interest in the place offers such strong opposition to the much advertised powers of time and change. It rained all through the afternoon until six, when it let up—apparently for my convenience. I thought of your riding home and generously hoped that you were not getting soaked.

I have not yet been able to get my mind down to work, but I can feel that the spirit is moving. My spirit, like my feet, moves slowly but generates a good deal of momentum. When it gets fairly started something is bound to happen.

The sun is out again now and everything is wet and shining, and there is a flavor of September in the atmosphere. September is everything to me that June was to Lowell. Though I don't ask Nature to lay her warm, or rather cool, ears down to earth. Or was it heaven that had ears? I fear I have got it all mixed up—and no man has a right to quote—unless he can quote straight. If "What is so rare" is one of your favorite passages, forgive me, I think it is pretty much like rot.

. . . For yourself, keep busy at something, but don't do very much work. If you can follow this advice you will be the happiest of all mortals who are managing a vacation.

II
DUST AND HEAT
(*Aetat.* 29–36)

TO DANIEL GREGORY MASON

71 Irving Place, New York City
30 October, 1899

. . . The competent bed-bug drove me out of my second resting place in Washington Square and I am here in a little box room where everything is new. My wall decorations consist of a red match box and a fifty-cent photograph of Beethoven which I bought the other day for the sake of having the presence of a fellow who did things without cars.[1] I am beginning to feel contented and settled though I confess to an occasional qualm for your den in Newbury Street. Let me hear from you from time to time.

I have just finished *Wuthering Heights* by Emily Brontë and feel as if I had digested a thunder-storm. It is a book of genius, but not the kind of genius that makes men grand. Read it when you feel dangerously cheerful and tell me what you think of it. It is crude and even amusing in its workmanship, clearness and elegance are left out, but there is force enough to run a saw mill. . . .

TO DANIEL GREGORY MASON

71 Irving Place
26 November, 1899

. . . Last week we had the Fourth Symphony of Brahms and it took hold of me like the jaws of something—something that never lets go. I heard it eight years ago in Boston but kept nothing of it but a big vague memory of the second movement. If I could hear it once a week for the next three months, I would pay the price of admission, even at the expense of apples. Speaking of apples. I have a permanent dago around the corner who sells me three big Northern Spies for five cents—the same as those I used to eat at home twenty years ago—before I ever questioned the unqualified greatness of Mr. Poe's "Raven"—and I have occasional nostalgic disturbances after eating them. I have tried sometimes to look on apples as a thing that we should outgrow—like circus lemonade—but I have not yet been able to put down the old bucolic appetite for Spies, Belfleurs (they should be Bell-Flowers), Baldwins, and Seek-no-Farthers. I never cared such a Devil of a lot for Kings and Greenings, but for the others I was always sore an-hungered. As I analyse my feelings while eating them, I have to confess that my edification is more than half-sentiment. The Virgilian *rusticus es* in me will not be killed. And on the whole I am not altogether certain that I wish to kill it.

I remember one rainy afternoon, the deuce knows how long ago, when I went down to the orchard with a tin pail and an umbrella and got Gravensteins. When I got back I washed off the dead grass and the mud and had a solitary orgy by the fire. After I had eaten about ten I began to blow scales on the clarinet. I have not a doubt but that I ate an enormous supper that night and read "The Raven" with an unaccustomed force, and I may have added "Lochiel's Warning" and the "Cataract of Lodore". The clarinet blowing, however, never amounted to much, and later when I had a machine of my own I never succeeded in getting anywhere with it. I could do "The Flying Trapeze" and "Abide With Me" pretty well, but I could never do the march in *The Prophet*—not because I couldn't finger it, but because I got tangled up in trying to read it. I couldn't get the tune through my head. I am glad you have shaken off the Harvard work, you give me a feeling that you are coming out all right. When you need recreation you might arrange Humperdinck—his music for the Xylophone.

TO JOHN HAYS GARDINER

71 Irving Place
March 25, 1900

It was very good of you to speak to Duffield; [1] and as long as your friendliness in this matter has nothing to do with a "job", I shall certainly have a talk with the man. When the time comes—I suppose you are beginning to wonder if it will ever come,—I'll let you send me a letter to him. You will not misinterpret my reference to a job. All I mean is that my performance in Cambridge [2] makes it utterly impossible for me to compromise your self-respect a second time. It was pretty bad, but you see I have only half a brain. You fellows who suffer from the disadvantage of having whole ones can hardly understand how it was possible for me to cut the figure I did and still be, in my own way, a creature of passable intelligence, and you may be sure that I appreciate your feelings. Even though your long-suffering fidelity to what there is of me—cerebrally speaking—reveals an element of something like desperate curiosity in your attitude, it does not occur to me to doubt that your friendliness is genuine and that you find in me, under favorable conditions, something to make you believe that I am not altogether an idiot. I am presuming not a little in saying this, for I know all about it—or think I do, which is just the same thing.

I am afraid that Miss Peabody did not give you a very eulogistic appreciation of me. Not long before you met her

I requested her not to dock the tail of her poetical horse—not in just those words, perhaps—and I had reason to believe that she did not value my remarks as she should have valued them. You see I got really after her, and I was afraid that I had hurt her feelings; but she came around last week with the most docile of all letters, and I have not felt since then that I was quite so violent as I thought. She has a great deal of talent and a good deal of confidence, but each of the two possessions is of a kind that needs to be agitated now and then. I fear I have a way of appointing myself too cheerfully to the post of arch-agitator, and I do it always with the best of intentions. I might add, incidentally, that I never lose consciousness of the fact that I am a perennial candidate for the same sort of treatment.

TO DANIEL GREGORY MASON

71 Irving Place
18 April, 1900

On the evening of the Eighteenth day of April, in the year of our Lord One Thousand Nine Hundred, I feel impelled to give you the dregs of my creative intelligence and to say that I am, as usual, a howling optimist. I am particularly optimistic just now because I am on the home stretch with *The Pauper*. It gags me to look at the twelve-hundred odd lines that have come back from the machine, but I have a satisfying consciousness of having done something and that's what makes me an optimist. By the time the thing has come back from six or seven publishers, I may be more rational, but for the present it pleases me to give myself a place among the possibilities. I am an economist, also, and I shall emigrate from this village in the near

future. Whether I go to Winthrop * * * or to Saxton's
River, Vermont (where a man can live on five dollars a week
and see trees), or to the island of Tristan da Cunha, where
they live and multiply without the interference of money,
I have not yet decided; but I shall go somewhere to finish
the other book and, in the course of a year, do the greater
part of another. Speaking of delectable islands makes me
think that I have been twice this spring to hear Tristan and
Isolde, which I maintain to be the only opera, as such, ever
written. All the rest of them are abortions and monstrosities
in one way or another—with the exception, perhaps, of Die
Meistersinger, which I shall not hear until I apply to President Eliot for a large pension on the ground of Permanent
Inability in the College office. I am glad to know that
Moody has written another poem [1] but I am sorry that he
calls it an ode. That, however, is his business, not mine. I
am keeping an eye out for the next *Atlantic*, and am wondering what the deuce the thing is like; for I could no more
get together a poem on the Philippines than I could write a
description of the human brain. All I know about the human
brain is that it seems to be indispensable and that it gets to
be damnably tired; and this is more than I know about the
right of our incomparable republic to make a game preserve
of the Philippines. My knowledge of politics is meagre and
my knowledge of Destiny is so small that it doesn't count.
I have to content myself with a jew's-harp and a bass-drum
and let the other fellow blow the trumpets. I have a pro-
phetic feeling that Moody has sounded a clear note—partly
on account of your word "magnificent" and partly on account of a way the man has of making laddered music spring
skyward from prophets' pillows and other kinds of music
do things in a way on which he seems to have the God-given
bulge, so to speak. How are you feeling? (When a man
says that, it is time for him to go to bed.)

TO DANIEL GREGORY MASON

71 Irving Place
18 May, 1900

While you are shamelessly pursuing literature on sybaritic brown paper, I am trying to do something with my Emerson and Erasmus sonnets. I enclose a partly made thing for your august analysis, and I beg of you to get after it as hard as you can. If you ask me to fix it, you will make me your enemy for the rest of your life, but if you merely tell me that it is rot I shall keep on esteeming you as heretofore. I wrote it with a pencil only because I have a childish, half-desperate notion that you may be able to read it in that form. I would write it on a slate if I had one.

Mr. Stedman is very much wound up by Moody's ode. We talked about the man for nearly an hour the other evening and I was mighty glad to know that the greater part of the poem is to go into the anthology which Mr. Stedman has been solidifying for the past three years—I say three, but it may be six. I believe my uncomfortable abstraction called "Luke Havergal" is also to be soused in anthological pickle—along with two or three others of the forlornly joyous breed.—*The Pauper,* or rather *Captain Craig*—for that is what I call him, now he is typewritten, is temporarily off my hands. Two friends of mine have read him and they are still friends of mine. More than this I cannot say for the present.

TO DANIEL GREGORY MASON

71 Irving Place
21 September, 1900

. . . You ought to see some of my prose. I am annoying all the gray-headed editors in New York with it, and I'm having lots of fun. Moody's Gloucester poem is better than his more splendiferous ode, I think. What else has he been doing? And what are you doing in the way of music?

Brahms never owned a piano—so they say. Always worked the manufacturers for them as an advertisement. Now if a cuss could only get a lyre with a thin horn (I think Moody is responsible for lyres with thin horns) in the same way it would be a grateful transaction—for then he wouldn't have to write bad prose and get himself scolded by gray-headed editors—although of course he would love the fun. As it is, things are balanced.

Have you read *Beauchamp's Career* yet? It's a part of everybody's education.

TO JOSEPHINE PRESTON PEABODY

Yonkers, 25 November, 1900

I have not had much time to think of *C. C.*[1] lately, but I appreciate all the friendly things you have to say of him and I sympathize with you in the matter of Wocky-Bocky.[2] If he is as bad to you as "something had, etc." is to me, we are quits. Personally I think him pleasant, if not mellifluous, though of course I may grow to see my mistake. In the meantime I'm afraid that you take him (C. C. not W. B.) rather too seriously. I think you put more of my own shortcomings into him than are there and somehow in the places where they are not at all. Otherwise you would like Wocky Bocky. He is a real being, by the way—or was (the poor devil is dead now)—and I used to go on the trail with him. This and the few lines where Killigrew stretches himself and lights his pipe are the only things in the book that are drawn directly from life. That particular part of Killigrew is now in the Library School at Albany, and is making an excellent recovery. I remember that I congratulated him when she turned him down, but I could hardly bring that into the book; I don't think much of carrying fact into fiction anyhow.—You ask me if I have heard anything definite from S. M. & Co.,[3] and I think, naturally, that you do so out of an incurable instinct for some sort of occupation.

Moody has arrived here with his Temperament—in New York, I mean—and the two have been trying to live in my old room at 71. They got along very well for about a week— to my surprise, for the place is not much more than enough for Falstaff's treble hautboy—and they concluded then that they would go out and find another mansion. They are doing very well now at Number 40, West 12th Street, where I expect to see them next Monday. I have been reading the *Masque*,[4] and I call it a pretty big thing; but I don't know how many will make anything more of it than a general attack on traditional theology. I must confess that the real scheme of it escaped me, and I fear that it will escape a good many others—which will be a disappointment to Moody, as I see that he takes the book very much in earnest. I do not wonder at all that he does, either; but I hope he feels glad somehow that he has got the thing off his hands. It proves beyond a doubt that the fellow has it in him to do remarkable things, and he ought therefore to be on good terms with himself; and I think he is, upon the whole, though I do not mean to imply that he shows any symptoms of the Swelled Head. I do not see how the book is going to sell to any extent, but I do see, without any difficulty, how it is going to help him a good deal. Perhaps Moody's greatest trouble lies in the fact that he has so many things to unlearn.

Apropos of delicate phrasing, why don't you tell me whether you like—i.e., whether you can stand—the observations of the chap in C. C.'s first letter about the pretty woman on horseback? I know well enough that they will not be tolerated by what Professor Hill calls "the better class of those who say 'he don't' ", but I have hopes that some others will enjoy it. It seems to me to be poetry, but I shall not be sure that it is until some creature of rarer fibre tells me so. . . .

TO DANIEL GREGORY MASON

Yonkers, 25 December, 1900

Your letter came as a welcome visitor on a somewhat bogus Christmas, and I will add that it came just as I was about to write an acknowledgment of your book [1]—which I am glad to own. I think your introduction is about what it should be, though I am inclined to question if you did not lay a little unnecessary stress now and then on Savage's personal limitations. You give me the impression of having been perhaps too careful not to overpraise a dead friend, and this leads me to fear that I may be too careful not to overpraise a living one. There are many good things among the poems and I am inclined to think that there are three or four at least that will take a permanent place; but I can't make myself believe, no matter how hard I try, that the man would have been happy if he had lived. There was too much of him (to epitomize what you say) to be satisfied.

Even the poet part of him was not quite enough to have kept the rest in harness. You have done a good work, and I think now that you did the best thing in not trying to sift the verses out any more than was absolutely necessary. One of the godlike things about me is that I can change my mind as easily as I can change my trousers—perhaps a little more so. For my trousers always stick on my damned heels.—In regard to the long letter which you wrote but did not send there is nothing for me to say except that if any suggestion of mine, or any safety valve of sympathy, can be of any worth to you, it is always ready. I have supposed that things were somewhat snarled with you, but of course I have not carried my supposition any farther than that. I appreciate your confidence in me, and I want you to know it; and at the same time I ask you to believe that I have always had a good deal of sympathy—more or less vague, but still of what I may call the solid sort—with your ambitions to do what you were born to do and with your difficulties, of which you say so little. Being such a cheerful abortion as I am in many ways, I suppose I can partly understand a few things that some other people cannot; and I have thought sometimes that my chief usefulness in the world lies in this faculty of mine to encourage a fellow man to shin up tall trees while I sit on the ground and tell him what an artist he is. Shinning—I hope the word is not strange to you—is the first of all the arts and I am beginning to fear that I have not done much of it. I cannot look back and feel honestly that I could have done more, but this feeling is rather a sorry poultice for the present and it isn't altogether an elixir for the future; but as long as I can see that the few real things that I have done are things that nobody knows about except myself I am willing to give the future a chance.

All this may seem irrelevant, but I am really trying to preach a sermon on the folly of measuring one's success too much in the scale of external evidence. The Ass-Demon of Quantity raises the devil with most of us and makes us forget that the test of a man is his willingness to measure himself by what he has tried to do—which is truly what he has done. It is right here somewhere that those "other things" begin to be added on, and one wonders where the deuce they come from. Forgive my throwing all this antiquated hay in your crib, but don't think I am keeping myself alive with the same crop. Remember, also, that I believe in the most modern of all oats, and that I am quite impervious to the trivial recriminations of little things like mixed metaphors. I began by watching another man go up a tree, and here I find myself a horse—which is well enough for Christmas in Yonkers. What you say of S. M. & Co. doesn't surprise me. I don't pretend to like Maynard's methods, or to believe that he can keep himself afloat if he continues to follow them, but still I shall let him publish *The Pauper* for the same reason that I should let him remove the Old Man of the Sea from my neck. If you can read this you will be fortunate.

TO JOSEPHINE PRESTON PEABODY

Yonkers, 1 January, 1901

I thank you for your good wishes and in return for them I will say that I hope you may live through the whole of the new century—if you wish to do so. In the year 2000 you will be, according to the Stedman system,[1] 12 years old, and your raven locks will be snowy white. You will be going about with an ear-trumpet and a gold-headed cane, and I suppose you will be telling all manner of people that they are looking "palely." . . .

Down in Riverdale, by the way, there is a fellow who plays

the viola like an escaped angel and I think I shall have to make him fiddle Mason's Irish song. It takes something in the way of fiddle to bring out one of those old airs, and Waldo [2] is always looking for them to make sandwiches of with Bach and the rest of them; and in this tune I fancy that I have a thing that will make him grow. Moody thinks Waldo's viola makes too many demands on one's nervous system, but I can listen to it for half a day at a time— which shows one of the many advantages of not having a temperament. I am glad to have you write as you do (throwing aside your remarks about yourself as superfluous) of the *Masque*. For I believe the thing is really great. It makes me feel funny with my *Captain Craigs*, etc., but I take comfort in the fact that the books are so ridiculously different that a comparison is hardly possible. Do not think that I took down all of your extravagant praise without a large allowance of salt. For that would be cruelty on your part.— What and where is the Colonial Theatre? I have not heard of it before, but I am glad to know about the panels and I shall look them up when I make my journey to Boston, which I am beginning to think of as a region of strange things. The strangest thing that has come from there recently is Maynard's naive statement that the long delay over my MS. was due to its great merit. I don't know whether he means the merit of the delay or of the MS. but in either case it would seem that our old friend Ananias was not such a talented fellow after all. But he appears to be much better underneath than I might have supposed, though I don't understand how he can keep going much longer—especially if he continues to paint the tops and edges of his books as he did the *Masque* and a novel called *Quicksand*. That sort of thing is really a crime.—I enclose a copy of my Song with the earnest request that you endeavor to tell me what is the matter with it. There is something that I have not cured even by throwing away twenty-four lines, which I did with joy at Moody's suggestion. If you can improve it by tearing out two more, do so by all means. You see I tried to do something "rather swagger" (I have been reading the Human Boy, which is a triumph) and I did not quite succeed. I shall print it, I suppose, but I can't pretend that I am half-satisfied with it. . . .

TO JOHN HAYS GARDINER

Yonkers, 17 January, 1901
I hope you are free from your troubles by this time and that you have found time to read at least a part of Wendell's [1] book. I have read pretty much the whole of it and I am now ready to wish that I had another book of the same size by the same man. This is a most prodigious compliment, as you see, but I make it without any hesitation. I don't wonder that you "plain people" are somewhat excited, nor do I think of any better testimony than this particular excitement for the fact that this book was needed. The sentimental Yankee is supposed to be a lover of truth, but I have observed that whenever the truth is thrown at him he is given to setting up a most singular howl. I am inclined to do a little howling of my own over the chapters on Emerson, but this inclination on my part may be due to "temper" rather than to intelligence, and therefore I'll try to keep it in. You see I have a sneaking fancy that if I had been living in the Brook Farm days, I should have borrowed a shovel or something and gone along. Please do not think, though, that I should do it today.

If you will read Moody's *Masque* I am sure that you will have a new opinion of the man. Barring six or eight scattered verses that are entirely damnable and unique in literature, the thing is an astonishing work of art and almost flawless in construction. The man has continued somehow to give unity, coherence, concreteness, and all the other things you people like to talk about, to the most difficult and unpromising material. You may call it a *tour de force* and say it is out of season, but you will have to confess that he has vitalized it according to modern methods and that he has made a modern poem of it. Now and then his imagination runs away with him, but that is said to be a good symptom in the young; and Moody, with all his pre-digested experiences, is not yet more than half so old as he thinks he is. If this has an unfriendly sound you may be sure that I do not intend it to have anything of the sort; for the fellow is in reality one of the most human and attractive of mortals. . . .

TO JOSEPHINE PRESTON PEABODY

Yonkers, January 30, 1901

Please do not think that I make light of your kind words in regard to my lyrical business and the *Captain*, for I assure you that I appreciated them very much. My only reason for calling them funny was that you left nothing else for me to say. So you will not be quite so lavish with your good words hereafter. You will pardon me for beginning with myself, and I hope you will not get mad when I tell you about my friend Henderson [1]—Chugg the chemist—who came down from Cambridge to stay over Saturday and Sunday with me. He was reading your book and saying good things about it, and it occurred to me that you might like to add him to your list for Cambridge. He is pretty young—class of '98—but he knows no end of chemistry. Fortunately, however, he knows and cares for other things, including poetry and Rembrandt's Dutchmen, and he can talk almost anything—from osmosis to Brook Farm. His strongest point is osmosis and I warn you and your sister to get him started on that subject in case you care to inspect him. He comes from Salem and he wears delicate red neckties. On the whole you would find him amusing, I think. His father and mother call him Lawrence, but his real name is Chugg. Incidentally he is a fierce critic—or he thinks he is, which is just the same thing. I hope you will let me send him credentials, for I am sure that you would like him. My only reason for all this preamble is the good one that letters of introduction are generally a bore. . . .

What do you hear from Torrence? I should like to know how he is getting along with his plays, but as he doesn't answer my letters I have no way of knowing. . . .

TO JOSEPHINE PRESTON PEABODY

29 East 22d Street, New York City
April 12th (I think), 1901

I have just sent a thousand lines of Imperishable Stuff to the typewriter and I feel a good deal better. Four hundred lines of it [1] are about two old men and a small boy, and the other six hundred are a woman who promised her dying spouse that she would never repeat the ceremony and six years after pledged herself to a fellow who kept a queer sort of journal and went to sleep on the day of his wife's funeral.[2] I don't know just how people will like this sort of thing, but I shall be interested to find out. I shall send the clergyman thing along in a day or two and by that time I shall feel that I have a book pretty well in hand.—I have heard nothing more in regard to S. M. Co. I took your letter as a gentle means of letting me know that they have gone into the hands of a receiver, but it appears from your last that my "insight" played a trick on me in accusing you of a charitable subtlety that you did not undertake. . . . My stern friend Pope,[3] who is down from Albany, approves of my new book with the exception of the Ballad—or rather "The Return of Morgan & Fingal", which I believe you have read: I mean the twenty-odd stanzas about the three chaps who ferried the dead girl and her half-crazy mother home through the storm and then went on with their hilarity as if nothing had happened. Maybe I didn't send it to you. If I did not I should like your criticism of one or two lines in it which trouble Pope on account of their directness. If a thing says what I mean it to say, and at the same time has rhythm and music in it, why shouldn't I use it even though I know that now and then a too conscientious critic will find fault with it? And the same fellow had the perseverance to read the whole of *Captain Craig* in MS. and at one sitting. Never had such a compliment in my life. I tried to assure him that he couldn't do it, but he did it and he did the same with the thousand lines I have referred to above. As a rule I make little or nothing of the praise of friends, but when a fellow goes through three thousand lines of my writing, I am compelled, with all my extreme modesty, to think there must be at least the germ of a reason for his doing so. . . . Mr. Stedman [4] was in amazingly good humor last evening and even went so far as not to disagree with me when I told him for the fortieth time that I have not the journalistic faculty. He appears to have given me up for good—as far as any practical brain power goes, and hereafter I trust that he will not be annoyed or disappointed at anything I do. He wants to see you, and he is going to look you up as soon as he knows you are here. So you may expect to see a rather small and very courteous old gentleman with white hair who may say all sorts of complimentary things—rather

too many, you may think at first—and tell you that you
are a Rare Spirit. He will say no end of things, in fact, and
he will mean all that he says. He believes that you are a sort
of lyrical miracle—if I may make such an epithet, and I
can assure you that Marlowe [5] will be nothing to him. . . .

TO JOSEPHINE PRESTON PEABODY

450 West 23d Street, New York City
June 25, 1901

I thank you for all of your suggestions in regard to the
Annandale things and I hope that I may be able to cure
myself of any threatened mannerism. At present my head is
too thoroughly filled with "other things" but I shall go over
those poems some day and try to remove the mark of Cain
to your complete satisfaction.—You may be interested in
learning that the admirable Ford [1] has taken upon himself,
voluntarily, the duties of my "literary execution". He is
going to see that the stuff is published sometime, and he is
therefore a rare soul. This means a big load from my shoul-
ders, naturally, and gives me different feelings in regard to
myself. Of course I shall keep on with the publishers unless
I find a way to print the books on my own account, but I
have no particular enthusiasm in the matter. My total lack
of all commercial instinct and my indifference to the little
whiff of newspaper notoriety that I might or might not get
from them leaves me not much more than the mere wish to
write what I have to write and to let it go its own way. If a
man's work is good for anything it will find a way to those
who read it; and if it isn't it won't. All this is so simple and
so obvious that it looks rather silly when it is down; but let
me tell you something that a man from the West told me
this spring: "In four or five years, my dear fellow, I am con-

fident that your name will be in the magazines." What is there for a fellow to say to relatively intelligent people who cannot understand anything? Perhaps he meant powder magazines—perhaps he didn't know what he meant. It is this sort of thing (and I get a good deal of it) that makes me wish sometimes that I lived in Madagascar. But I shouldn't like that, either; for then I should have no apples or *Tristan and Isolde.* I can't get along much without T. & I. and apples—which goes to show, no doubt, that something is not right with me.

There is nothing for me to tell you about people except that Torrence has finished his play and that Mrs. Stoddard [2] gave me such a terrible talk two or three weeks ago that I have not dared to go there since. R. H. S. was not visible and as a natural consequence I fared pretty badly. I don't think she heard anything that I said, but on the other hand I doubt if that really made any difference. She didn't give me a chance to say much. Stedman has moved himself to Bronxville, and I shall not see him again till fall. . . .

Sometime ago you liked a little cat poem which I tore out of a *Spectator* and sent to you, and it has occurred to me that you may like this performance by the same writer. I don't understand all the natural history in it, but perhaps you will. If you don't you will like the flavor of the verses. I'll send you my Klondike ballad as soon as I get it fixed up and copied and defy you to find any other things in it. It's a pretty amusing piece of literature, I fancy, and it ought to be a good antidote for the thermometer even if it isn't very good poetry. I'm not sure that it is poetry [at] all. I'm not particularly sure that I have yet found out what poetry is, anyhow. If you know I wish you would tell me.— Waldo sends me the enclosed slating of the *Masque,*[3] which is altogether flippant and one sided.

TO DANIEL GREGORY MASON

450 West 23rd Street
July 7, 1901

. . . It is very good of you to ask me to spend a part of
the sweltering season with you, but I must say again that
it will be utterly impossible for me to do so. Under different circumstances nothing would give me greater pleasure,
and I say this in the hope that you will believe me. You are
right in fancying that New York is not the ideal American
summer resort, but there is an empty flat in Harlem again
to which I am invited by a good fellow who really wants me
to come, and as I see no reason or excuse for not accepting
his invitation I shall in all probability go there this week.
Sometime in the future I may be able to live and move and
have the being of a civilized biped again, but the devil only
knows when that time will come. In the meantime, I continue to be a vagabond and to squeeze out a modicum of
metrical stuff that may or may not be amusing to somebody
when I am boxed up and stowed away. I don't take this
course from any silly notion of "art for art's sake", but because I find no other. I am not quite so damned lazy as my
friends think, either. I am simply incomplete and made up
as far as I am made at all of what must have been left over
after the manufacture of some sixteen or seventeen fellows
who were more fortunate perhaps than I am. By this description, if by no other, I am a man of parts—some of them
pretty little, and none of them fastened together very well.
This is where Moody is big while I am small. He can do the
world's work for the admirable reason that he has a brain.
There is a possibility of his growing up someday and writing
like Shakespeare—or maybe like a new Ibsen without smoky

spectacles. Up to this time he has been a little afraid of the light; but, as I told him myself, he will not show the world what is in him until he comes to Book Fourth or Book Fifth. He may have thought that I was presuming on my vaga-bondage when I said it, but that is no great matter. . . .

TO DANIEL GREGORY MASON

450 West 23d Street
26 September, 1901

I have just moved back again to my old cell in Twenty-third Street and I find to my huge delight that the place has been painted pea-green—apparently in expectation of my return. Everything is so damnably clean that I don't yet feel quite comfortable; and yet clean is hardly the word either, for there was never any dirt, per se, the room was merely out at the elbows. Now I have gone and glorified myself with a new writing table—which was a moral crime on my part—and I feel much better. I have had two small inspirations already, and I am likely to have another before dinner-time. Moral: go to John Wanamaker's and buy a table—particularly if you can't afford it. In that case it will be much more satisfactory. You see I have not forgot the lesson I learned when I spent two dollars of a final four for a couple of opera tickets—to the peanut gallery, of course. If I can keep on doing this sort of thing, there may be a chance for my success.

It is good to know that the A. P.[1] has brains enough to send Moody's book into a second edition. When I received your word to that effect I was tempted to write to him at once and beg him to take out "by God's ring-finger stirred" —which is, with all respect to genius, really damnable. It is so bad, in fact, that only a genius could do it; and I am rather sorry now that I did not write, if only for the piety of the performance. From the twenty or so who have spoken to me of the book I have heard nothing but praise with a big P. All, however, make an exception of "The Menagerie" —not because they do not like it in itself but because it seems to be hopelessly out of place. I have a notion that I shall agree with them by and by, but the thing is so confoundedly clever that I hate to see it go. I still cling to my first belief that "The Daguerreotype" and "The Departure" reach the finest and highest quality of anything in the book. —There are a few faint possibilities coming up on my own horizon, but I do not say anything about them at present. C. C. has been turned down by five houses, but he is still on the march. His trousers are pretty badly frayed, and his general appearance seems to be more and more disreputable on each return; but perhaps that is all right. He is a sort of disreputable cuss, anyhow, as you know.

My only backward criticism of *Esther Waters* is on the possible ground of too much "realism" in the way of unnecessary details. It is a great book and one that ought to do a good work in the world. From the artist's point of view I cannot place it along with Hardy's *Jude the Obscure*, but it has a message without being a sermon and for that reason will live. Nearly all of Hardy will die, I think, though I dislike to think of the funeral of *The Return of the Native*. I should call *Jude*, with all its misery, his one book that is true.

I hope before long to know that you are in a better way to see a glimpse of some sort of light through your cypress trees. None of us can live always in a swamp, and for this reason I hope you will try to find some way out, if you have to go to New Zealand.[2] I think of going there myself.

450 West 23d St.
December 9, 1901

Why in the name of Eben Holden did you put an exclamation point after "when the other men are done with it"? I don't like to find fault, but when you go to work deliberately to hurt the feelings of your readers, and tell them in this left-handed way that This Is A Good One, you ought not to be surprised if they snarl a little. J. M. Barrie refers, through a woman character, to that dreadful class of authors who do not put exclamation points after their jokes, and he might have referred at the same time to the still more dreadful class who do not put them after their Sublime Passages. Fortunately you are one of these, but even this saving grace is not enough to make up for the particularly unpardonable offense I have referred to. If you try to defend it I shall know that you are juggling with your literary conscience and refer you forthwith to Professor Bates, who will agree with me. If she does not, she must be removed and drawn down to the lower circle where mistaken souls are reading F. C. Burnand's *Happy Thoughts* and calling them funny.—I believe that this is the only serious criticism I have to make in the way of censure unless I make myself so obnoxious as to be entirely honest about Act V. Of course all Act V's are, in the nature of things, pretty bad—in tragedies, I mean—and for this reason I don't feel like saying much. But I think you might do well to keep the subject in mind and even to entertain the possibility of rewriting sometime in the future. I suppose this will make you mad, but as my chief mission in this life appears to be that of a very long animal who barks and snarls when he means to make all sorts of good-natured and affectionate noises, perhaps I ought not to mind your rage. In any case, however, do not forget that you have written a tremendously good thing. I have no quarrel whatever with the first four acts and by this I mean 45 times more than I say. Whenever I try to praise anything I tie myself in hard knots and generally leave my victim in doubt as to whether I know what I am talking about. I can damn a work of art pretty effectively when I am in the mood and on the other hand I can appreciate one; but when it comes to putting my appreciation in words I am always sorry I spoke. I'm just the same with gratitude—so much so that there are people in the world who think I am mostly an hippopotamus; and they may be right. Still I can say, or try to say, that your *Marlowe* has a vital quality that lifts it altogether out of the common order of "exceptional verse" and compels me to judge it by the highest standards or not to judge it at all. One would hardly think of applying the test to anything by Stephen Phillips, or, for that matter, to anything in the shape of a play that has been written in English by anyone since Browning. I say since Browning, but I am not sure that I know just what I mean by saying it; for his plays— so called—are so deadly dull that I have always found it next to impossible to read them. Whatever *Marlowe* is, it is interesting first of all; and it has more real dramatic feeling in it than I should be able to find in *Herod, Becket,* and *Colombe's Birthday* rolled into one. I have never read *Becket,* by the way, and I see no reason why I ever should. Tennyson is so much worse than Browning that I am willing to be content with what I have tried to read of his other things in "dramatic form"—an expression which must mean something or nothing. I wonder sometimes if a court stenographer writes in dramatic form. Anyhow I am sure that a fairly good trial for dog-stealing would make a better play than *Luria.*—I am looking for good reports of *Marlowe,* and if I do not find them I shall have but one more assurance of the asininity of critics. Also I hope to have a good report in regard to your health.

TO MRS. LAURA E. RICHARDS

450 West 23d Street
Jan. 1st, 1902

If I have a chance to do what I have now pretty definitely laid out, I shall at least have made an attempt to do something worth while. I shall please the people more or less— some time—but I doubt very much if I do anything at present more than write. I have so little stomach for breathing on the boots of publishers, and so little of what is called tact—

TO MRS. LAURA E. RICHARDS

450 West 23d Street
Jan. 18, 1902

I thought Shiras [1] and the Klondike [2] were rather the best things in the book—all of which goes to show that a fellow is not a very good judge of his own performances. I'll do you a whole bundle of Twilight Songs some day, but I can't do them just now on account of the preponderance of daylight which illuminates this Blessed City. The jingle will come in time, however, and then doubtless I shall care more for it. By the way, there's jingle in "The Klondike" if you get my notion of quantity—likewise in the wilderness thing,[3] which some people cannot read on account of its "lack of restraint."

I am writing now more than I am reading, perhaps, and possibly I am doing work that will please you more or less by virtue of its jingle. It will be a book of something like fifty poems [4]—all "poetry" more or less, and nearly all in rhyme. The deuce only knows what I shall do with it when it is done, or when it will be in that condition. Probably not for two or three years, for I see that it will be interrupted by something different. What I don't see is, how a man can write this sort of stuff and locate himself with anything like definiteness more often than once in the twentieth part of a century. Probably more than half of the reputable failures in literature come from trying to do this.

Von Moody,[5] the pessimist man-child who branded himself the best of living poets with "The Daguerreotype," is coming here in a day or two, and I trust he will have some new sort of ochre to throw on me. It might be good for me if a little of it were to stick, but I fear that is impossible just at present. My poetical overcoat is too smooth—not to say "shiny". Moreover, I am what I am; and therefore I have my own paint-pots to dabble with. Blacks and grays and browns and blues for the most part—but also a trick, I hope, of letting the white come through in places.[6]

TO MRS. LAURA E. RICHARDS

450 West 23d Street
[No date, probably Feb. 1902]

Each new experience I have with these people [publishers] makes me more and more inclined to write in my own way and trust to the powers that be that some of it may be worth while to somebody. A dozen lines of real matter is worth so much more to me than a dozen volumes of "creditable verse" that I shall hardly be able to capitulate a great deal to suit those who control the trade lists. But on the other hand I hope I shall always be willing to throw a

thing away when I see that my own whim has run off with
me—as in the case of Shiras. When I told you that I thought
it was one of the best things in the book I was simply hanging on to the tail of the whim, knowing all the time that I
should be glad to let go before long. So you see I am not
"contrary", or more than ordinarily unreasonable. About
half of the new book [1] is, relatively speaking, rubbish. Two
thirds of most books of its kind are made up of the same
material—which figuring gives me a slight advantage provided I am right. All this is a matter of chance and temperament, however, and I may come in the end to care nothing
for Sainte-Nitouche and Aunt Imogen. Personally I should
call the woman and wife affair [2] the best I have ever done
or am likely to do, but next year I may throw it away.

TO MRS. LAURA E. RICHARDS

450 West 23d Street
March 9th, 1902

If I am spared for another half of a decade I expect to do
a book of mixed up short things that will probably please
you, and incidentally a Trilogy. (Trill = a pretty noise and
orgy = the very devil of a time. I turn it into *ojy* for pho-
netico-linguistic reasons which you will understand.) It isn't
to be a trilogy for the stage, but altogether for the shelf,
and—may the Lord be good to you always—in my own particular blank verse, with a spatter of rhyme here and there.
It will be as comical as the deuce and, somewhat unlike
C. C., almost wholly objective. If the time comes for me to
do Alcibiades, Owen Glendower, and three or four other
gentlemen, you will find the original ME as far away from
the text as you find it now in little John Evereldown. I call
him little because he isn't big. He is merely John Tarbox

plus a superannuated projection of . . . I go into these details only because of your persistent failure to "understand".
Aaron Stark, on the contrary, has nothing whatever to do
with the late N. M. Whitmore, or with anyone else. No more
has Shiras, who seems to be a source of constant trouble
to you. I have come to the conclusion, by the way, that he
doesn't amount to anything in his present dress, and I am
inclined to look on him as a providential warning in the
way of style. He points back to *C. C.* with a long skinny
finger and says, "Thus far, etc." . . .

I hope you have never doubted that he (*C. C.*) is a gentleman, and I hope too that you will not mislike him for his
theory that it is possible to apply good natured common
sense even to the so-called serious events in life.

TO JOSEPHINE PRESTON PEABODY

Boston, August 14, 1902
I am not sending much in return for your two long letters,
but as you know that I can't write letters any more—for
the present, anyhow—you will not make the wicked mistake
of thinking me in any way indifferent. I don't think I quite
agree with you in your relative estimation of human beings
and heather, and I will even go so far as to believe that this
same heather will send you home thinking rather more than
ever before of the previously despised who are trotting all
over the earth and apparently to no great purpose. There
is something in them, or they wouldn't keep on trotting so
long. . . .

I think you have made me understand pretty well how
this world looks to you, and you have surely given me the
feeling that you would not have had it look otherwise even
if you could have ordered it. All your crying, if I may refer

to it, was probably of more value to you than anything that
anybody will ever say about it. It is best for us all to know
how pitifully close to earth we are, and it is particularly
good—now and then, not too often—that one should learn
it through heather and such like, or through the sunset on
Stoughton Hall in October, or maybe through the sight of
a page of printed Greek verse. I don't know that it makes
any great difference how it comes. To me—and I'm rather
glad of it—it will come as well as any other way through
the smoke and sky-scrapers behind Brooklyn Bridge—or
from lower Fifth Avenue after dark. But not much, somehow, from anything here in Boston. What little of New
England was ever in me has been pretty much extirpated—
though of course my arms and legs and nose music when I
talk will always proclaim the state of my birth. That brings
me to the point again. So too does an automobile, if it is a
good one; likewise a machine like the Deutschland. Thank
you for the twigs.

TO JOSEPHINE PRESTON PEABODY

450 West 23d Street
23 January, 1904

. . . You spoke of me in the subway as if you thought me
the most miserable object on earth—I mean under it. Believe me when I tell you again that I am nothing of the
sort, even though the life may have a paralyzing effect on
my letters. I fear that something had, long before I under-
took this work. If you have any sympathy to spare, for
heaven's sake think of poor Torrence under the eye of J.
L. Gilder,[1] reading bad manuscript from morning till night,
or of poor D. G. M.[2] trying to fit his immortal soul (in a
cold room at that) into the mould approved by the sons

of the Reverend Lyman Abbott—not to mention Hamilton
W. Mabie.³ Think of me only as a well meaning and well
wishing friend with one little wheel somewhere in back of
his cranium that never got started. It may start yet. And
then there may be some fireworks. Fizz! I don't know.

TO JOHN HAYS GARDINER

450 West 23d Street
31 January 1904

After thanking you most sincerely for your last letter I
can only say that I believe in the subway—for the present
at any rate. If my mind is not large enough to include a
few months of monotony and dirt, surely it is not large
enough for you to think about. As for money, let me answer
you that I am getting along very well.—If I were to come
out of my hole now I should feel that I was making the
mortal blunder of my life. Some time in the future, when
my new book is ripe, I may humbly let you help me out,
if it seems necessary. But in the meantime I know that I
am right in the course that I have taken.

TO JOHN HAYS GARDINER

450 West 23d Street
15 September 1904

Thank you for your letter and for your very friendly
invitation. Under other conditions I should surely take advantage of it, but I am sorry to say that it will be out of
the question this time—for reasons that I need not go into
at greater length than to say that I am not travelling at
present. I got out of the subway a month ago, as you heard

through Mrs. Richards, and I am willing to say that I am rather better on the whole for the experience. I shall soon be at work again in my old unreasonable way and in the course of time I shall have another book to my credit or discredit, as the case may be. Sometimes I am inclined to look with envy at any fellow who has an enthusiasm for anything so practical and immediately advantageous as running a peanut stand or swallowing swords. If I were to go into the peanut business I should burn more than I sold. If I were to swallow a sword the results might be more satisfactory to some of my friends, though I might not enjoy the process any more than I did the subway. I write this in the greatest good humor, even in the face of all the things that I know about myself. For, among other things, I know that I can keep on waiting for some time longer in the dark. It may be worth while, or it may not, but anyhow it seems to be the only work that I can come within a twelve-inch gun shot of doing at all. The present day disregard of everything save dynamics and dollars does not worry me in the least. If I happen to be ground to pieces in the hopper, I still have faith in the pieces. One of the things that gives me faith is the knowledge that I have had a few friends like you. I don't know that I have any right to assume that even these friends are going to believe in me very much longer, but whatever they do they cannot take back what they have already given. This is where I have an advantage over them.—I am feeling very well nowadays and I hope to bring something to pass before another winter is over. I take up Italian as a recreation and find it very good fun.

Let me thank you once more for the invitation that I cannot accept and for many other words and acts of yours that I cannot forget.

TO JOSEPHINE PRESTON PEABODY

76 Pinckney Street, Boston
26 January, 1905

I have read *Man and Superman* but I have nothing new to say of Shaw—or Pshaw, to use your improvement. To me he is still the same illogical composite of red rags and white corpuscles. I enjoy him for the moment out of all reason and then he is gone. In this instance he seems to have dressed himself out as Taurus and to have tied the rags to his own horns. He deserved all that you gave him,[1] but I am wondering now whether your sleep-destroying fancy was really worth while. Still, you must have made the Inframan uncomfortable, and no doubt that did him good. I am certain that it did you good, and that it did as much for several others. On the whole I am more than ever inclined to be sorry for Shaw: not on account of your attack, but on account of his last and most elaborate exposition of his complete futility. On this point you will think me soft, but I remain mortally sorry for a man of genius who cannot see that two and two do not make three —not to speak of five.

Also I remain

Your obedient servant
Hank Felio (not Figlio)

III
ARRIVAL
(*Aetat.* 35–57)

1 Yarmouth Street (Boston)
April 11, 1905

Some time ago I was surprised to receive a pleasant note from President Roosevelt, speaking well of my books and showing clearly that someone had been at work upon him. This note was soon followed by offers of employment in strange lands—to wit, in Montreal and Mexico—which I could not see my way to accept. Now he understands my situation, and I may or may not hear from him again. In many respects I am placed fortunately as I am, in that I have about two-thirds of my time to myself.[1] I have told him this, making it clear at the same time that if I could have more congenial work, with more pay and the same amount of leisure, I should be happy to get it. Were I not cursed with the poetical microbe, of course everything would be different. In fact, I should never have heard from him at all.

All this is in the way of saying that I thank you very much for what you have done in the matter. I cannot find out from Mr. Moody just how far he is implicated, as he contents himself with being facetious at my expense, after the manner of one who can well afford to do so. Will you kindly see that he gets his share of my gratitude? For even though nothing should come of it, I shall always remember this episode as one of those pleasant and unexpected things that come about as frequently as the Phoenix. I am quoting Schopenhauer apropos of the critic. He adds that the Phoenix comes once every five hundred years. All of which is amusing, but not to the purpose.

TO CRAVEN LANGSTROTH BETTS

1 Yarmouth Street, Boston
April 18, 1905

I have just received a letter from Mrs. C. in which she tells me that you are thinking of closing your establishment and living by yourself. I wonder if you will pardon me if I venture to hope that you will not spend too much time in thinking about it? You deserve your freedom, if ever a man did and you ought to have it. I have thought about it a great deal during the past two or three years and very likely I have been remiss sometimes in letting you know it. All this is only in the hope that you may soon have a den of your own and another for your sister. I have two cousins, brother and sister, who have lived together so long that I don't like to think about them. They are so much like married mummies that the thought of them makes me weep. I have no fear of your becoming like one of them, but I have a great fear of your losing that simple joy of living for which you have—or at any rate appear to have—such a God-given genius. Don't throw away the rest of your life, even if the change does make some disturbance in the lives of others. There is nothing in the law or the prophets that says a man must crucify himself to please his relations. I suppose I ought not to write this but I'm damned if I can help it.—If ever I get hold of any money, and there are small symptoms of such a thing, my first selfish dissipation will be to pay back (I don't like that way of putting it) some of the life that I owe to you. The opportunity may never come but we'll wait and see. If T. Roosevelt keeps on offering me two thousand dollar jobs that I don't want, I can't say what may happen. The trouble with me is that I want to live in New York. I can't feel at home anywhere

else. I have more than half a mind to get my shoes tapped
and go to Washington as soon as T.R. comes back from the
bear country. He says he wants to see me, and that he
doesn't want me to leave the country; so perhaps he can
land me in New York. Also, perhaps I may never hear from
him again. . . .

TO MRS. LAURA E. RICHARDS

United States Customs Service, Port of New York
June 5, 1905

Madam:

In reply to your letter of the second instant I have to say
that bananas and skeletons may be imported free of duty.
I regret to inform you that there is a duty of ten (10) per
centum on baked ant's eggs.

Respectfully,

E. A. Robinson

P. S. I am not in buttons—nor am I a Special Agent. I don't
yet see why I should be, but that may be explained.

TO MRS. LAURA E. RICHARDS

Special Agent Treasury Department
New York, August 7, 1905

The soulless Secretary of the Treasury has taken away
my steamboat and given me poor quality of paper in the bar-
gain. That steamboat was more than half of all that I had
in the world—in fact it was the only thing connected with
the United States Customs Service that was at all worth
while. Therefore the Secretary removed it. His dinner dis-
agreed with him sometime ago and since then he has been

dreaming that he is going to be the next President. All this is pretty nice on my part, for I assume it to be true that there is in him something that is as human as a stomach. You may think from my literary style that I have been reading the Holy Scriptures for relief, but I have not been reading them. On the contrary, I have been reading Torrence's monumental poem for the September *Atlantic,* by means of which he hopes to leap into immortal glory and leave Moody in the shadow, swearing. I don't think that he will quite do it, but he will do enough to make some thousands of people rub their eyes.

TO MRS. LAURA E. RICHARDS

[1905, undated]
The strenuous man has given me some of the most powerful loafing that has ever come my way.[1] Sometime there is going to be something to do—otherwise there would be no Custom House. As it is I look out upon Wall Street and see men going to their ruin and to their luncheons. It is a sad life. If my next book turns out pessimistic you are to attribute the fact to T. R., not to me. By nature I am jovial and sunny but I can't continue so unless there is crime in the world to cheer me up and give me something to do. I am (along with 13 others) the victim of other men's good conduct. If you are really a friend of mine you will go abroad at once and smuggle something. There is a duty of twenty cents a pound on nails.

Yours Very Truly

[Postscript]
I live at 450 West 23rd Street.

TO DANIEL GREGORY MASON

United States Customs Service, Port of New York
July 22, 1908

Under a new system and a new Boss my chief duty as a pillar of the government appears to consist in remaining a prisoner in Room 408. This is particularly rotten just now, as I am in a mood for work (work with me means studying the ceiling and my navel for four hours and then writing down perhaps four lines—sometimes as many as seven and again none at all) while there is just enough going on here, not to mention all hell outside, to keep my poor relic of a brain in a state that suggests nothing to me at the moment unless it be a state of semi-agitated punk. Yes, punk's the word with me; and it will be for some time to come unless I can contrive to hypnotize my chief officer into an appreciation of my place in nature. If I come in some afternoon and find him waving a "phony" invoice in one hand and Old Doctor Moody's *Masque of Judgment* in the other, I shall know that I have the right kind of an eye for him. Don't let my apparent inertness lead you into supposing that I am as mud in the hands of my immediate superiors, for there are other elements at work. As a matter of fact my three years in this business have not been, for the most part, years to make a fellow grow young. There is no need of my going into particulars. On the other hand don't you make the mistake of supposing that I have failed, or do fail, to appreciate my devilish good luck in landing here. My chief concern is a fear that I may turn out a disappointment to my friends and to T. R., who must be wondering—if he finds time—how long it takes a man to write a hundred pages of verse. It does not, in fact, take long to write a hundred pages of verse, but unfortunately, there is only a visual resemblance between verse and the other thing. For quantity (I mean size) I do not myself care a damn; but a fellow has to be dead before the public understands that a dozen titles are quite enough to string wires on that will reach through ten times as many centuries—perhaps. I don't know about my metaphor, nor do I know that I have ever done anything that the future will require, but I do know that those things I have done are my own (to use the world's nonsense) and that they have to be done in my way. If they go by the board, they will go because I could not build them any better.—Now that this exquisite bit of drivel is out of my system, I'll have a smoke.

Hurrah for crime—as Burnham[1] used to say,

Yours to command

TO RICHARD WATSON GILDER

United States Customs Service, Port of New York,
December 22, 1908

Since writing my hurried note of something like a fortnight ago I have been living with your book; and I wish now to repeat my sincere thanks to you for sending it. While nearly everything in it was familiar in a general way, I found, as a result of a more leisurely and intimate acquaintance with your work, now brought together in one volume, that the distinction and originality of the poems are perhaps even more apparent and satisfying than when they were scattered. It must give you a sense of comfortable triumph to know that your position in literature is assured beyond all question and that it is so honorable and so high. You will remember that I am writing as a younger man to his elder, and I am sure that you will excuse anything that may seem like naiveté in my attempt to express an admiration that is to be taken for what you think it worth, and in no sense as an accompaniment of my natural gratitude to you for your friendliness on many occasions in the past.

When I used to read your poems twenty years ago in Maine I little supposed that I was ever to meet the man who wrote them—still less did I suspect that I was ever to be under such pleasant and life-long obligations to him as I have lately experienced—in more ways than one.

Putting aside your past-mastery of technique—the praise of which would at this late date be banal—I admire most your willingness to look life in the face without resorting to the nauseating evasions of the uncompromising "optimist." The predominance of this willingness to be honest, with never the suggestion of surrender—or even of weariness—is to my mind the most admirable thing in life or in art—provided always that the artist has the faculty of being interesting. To be more concrete I will say I have long thought "Non Sine Dolore" not only interesting but exciting—and this is only one poem of thirty or forty of which I could say as much.

Yours sincerely, and always with gratitude and admiration,

TO LOUIS V. LEDOUX

545 Carlton Avenue
Brooklyn, July 22, 1909

If you will let me know which day will be convenient I'll come to New York and have a lunch-talk with you. I expect to leave these parts for an indefinite time before long and should hate to go without another sight of you. I got my "death-warrant" a few days after I saw you last time. Loeb is like the Heathen Chinee in that his methods are damned peculiar. Still, he has talent.

TO CRAVEN LANGSTROTH BETTS

Chocorua, New Hampshire
July 19, 1910

I was sorry not to be able to see you again before my somewhat precipitate flight from New York, but I found a door open for me and I felt that I couldn't stand it any longer. I fled to the Fall River boat Saturday afternoon and before I knew it I was buttoning my coat. Now I am down here in the woods with mountains all around me and no excuse for not working on a book that may, if it comes off, be both palatable and profitable. I shall know myself better in a day or two and be more at ease with nature. This place is a heavy dose for a neophyte but I see that I am going to like it. My only fear is that I may like it too well and so become too lazy to care whether I do anything or not. We shall see. Anyhow I hope that we may get together again in the fall. Be good. Yours always

TO LOUIS V. LEDOUX

Care T. H. Bartlett, Esq.
Chocorua, New Hampshire
July 20, 1910.

. . . I have a mountain here entirely of my own—so far as I can make out—and it comforts me in many ways. Also, it comes over me that Vickery's [1] psychology is sound—a point

upon which one or two have differed. Forgive me for referring to myself as if I were in McGillicuddy's Family Classics
—I did not mean to revert quite so abruptly to my own little
doings in the section where "sobs of the sensitive nine heave
upon Helicon's hump." It's the effect of the mountain air.
You had better come up here. It beats John Street all hollow
—but I won't rub it in. Besides it isn't going to last very
long. Nothing does but sorrow and Sir Charles Grandison.
By the way, did Abbott seem to know what I am driving at
in T.R. or did he disagree with it with some degree of intelligence? I have encountered so much rotten imbecility in the
way of failure to get my meaning that I am beginning to
wonder myself if it may not be vague. But I won't have it
anything worse than obscure, which I meant it to be—to a
certain extent.

Write me a letter whenever you feel charitably inclined.
Such a heavy dose of nature after all these years makes me
feel like reaching out, so to speak, for an occasional reassur-
ing hand.

TO MRS. WILLIAM VAUGHN MOODY

Chocorua, New Hampshire
July 29, 1910

You will see from this that I am in one of Will's
old haunts—up here in the semi-wilderness with old Mr.
Bartlett [1] who wishes to be remembered most violently. He
is just the same as ever—only a little older. His chief excitement in life consists in killing flies during meals and
swearing in a most piratical manner when he gets one. He
has lost little of his old energy and none of his profanity—
for which one is to be grateful.

In spite of your veiled warning I regret to report I have

written two chapters of the novel—if it may be called one, being a rehashing of an impossible play, with some added frills—and that I am ass enough to be rather pleased with what I have done. Of course this means that I have entered the Valley of the Shadow. If the October book of verse should by any chance amount to anything, the novel will undoubtedly knock it on the head, and serve it right. I ought to be willing to be a freak forever, and not try to make money. . . .

TO LOUIS V. LEDOUX

Chocorua, August 20, 1910

As I was out this morning, a-sniffing of the mountain air, I became filled with a hope that you might often come up here for a day or two. There is a hotel half a mile away and half an hour's ride from the Mount Whittier R.R. station, where you will get off if you come. I don't know how much you would get out of it but I have no doubts on my own side. It's only a short ride from Boston—$3.16—or you can go direct from New York and get here in the morning. . . .

As for early rising, you may see me, in your mind's eye, Horatio, getting up a little before eight any morning and working seven hours a day. If ever you read the novel you will be sorry that I did not lie abed all day.

Yours sincerely
P. Vickery, Esquire,
(If it must be, I may as well
let the mountain stay as it is.)

P.S.
"So they soon embarked, and sat upon the benches, sitting orderly, and smote the gray sea water with their oars." [1]

TO PERCY MACKAYE

Chocorua, October 17, 1910

Your telegram has just come. I cannot say that I am greatly surprised or that the death of Moody [1] was not the most merciful thing that could happen. I am sure that we both felt that the real man was gone when we saw him—I for the last time—that afternoon at Port Chester. Well, he did enough to give him his place among the immortals, and I believe that he did no man an injury while he lived.— Therefore, feeling as I do that there was nothing more for him in this life, I say that we ought to be glad that he lived, glad that we could know him, and glad that he is now done with pain. If this sounds cold, you know me too well to mistake it.

We shall have more to say when we see each other again.

TO MRS. WILLIAM VAUGHN MOODY

Chocorua, October 17, 1910

I have just received Percy MacKaye's telegram about Will. I cannot possibly say anything now more than to express my deepest sympathy for you at such a time as this. Thank God he lived to do his work—or enough of it to place him among the immortals. But you are not thinking of that now. Please accept these few clumsy words as you know that I would have them accepted, and forgive my inopportune note of the other day.

I hope that I may see you again sometime, and perhaps make you understand more clearly how fully I realize what you, and the world, have lost.

Peterborough, July 26, 1911

You did me a good turn when you pointed me in the direction of this place. I look out on stone walls and an old-fashioned rickety barred gate and about a dozen cows—to say nothing of the best maple trees that I ever saw in my life—and I was born in the land of maples. Taking everything together I am several degrees better off than I deserve to be, and I can only hope that I shall manage to do something that will eventually make things a little more square than they are now. But I won't harp on unpleasant subjects. I am glad to be able to say that I shall not have to bother you during the summer except to the extent of letting you know that I should be mighty glad to hear from you at any time. My life here, with all its silent attractions, is not exactly exciting, and therefore letters are more than ordinarily welcome.

TO LOUIS V. LEDOUX

Lower House
Peterborough, New Hampshire
[Date on Postmark, July 28, 1911]

I have been here for nearly two weeks and am still staring at stone walls as if I had never seen one before. I have seen thousands of them but I don't believe that I ever quite appreciated them. They were too near, I fancy, and there were too many of them. A week ago I got down to work and wrote three chapters of another novel. Just why I cannot say, for it appears, if I am to believe the Scribners, that my other one is too difficult and too far off the popular key to warrant their undertaking its publication. I don't know what they mean, but suppose they mean something. By the time I have finished the other, I may go back to poetry—which is always profitable and popular when compared with the kind of prose that I seem destined to write. I must be a damned fool, for to me the stuff seems as easy as lying—whatever faults in metrics it may possess. . . .

TO LOUIS V. LEDOUX

Peterborough, August 14, 1911

Thank you for Miss Sinclair's[1] address. Hagedorn ought to find her with it eventually. If I were you I should not spend a great deal of time in worrying about the criticism of any man, whatever his personal attractions may be, who is satisfied with "Comrades".[2] It may be that I am venomous on the subject of that poem but most certainly it does get on my nerves. So does my new book; having just finished the eighth chapter, I am inclined to wonder what the devil I think it is that I am doing anyhow. Houghton and Mifflin have the other, but I doubt if they will have it very long.

I shall be glad to see Torrence when I go back to New York—if I go. My future is, if possible, a bit more interesting and uncertain than ever. The wolf is keeping quiet for the present but I know that the brute is licking his chops behind some stone wall, or, at the farthest, somewhere in the neighborhood of Sixth Avenue and Washington Place. This is a beauchus country. I know that I am telling the truth, for I can see it—the country, not the truth—through my window. There are to be three concerts in the woods here this week and they may shake some of the dust of approaching senility out of my doddering brain.

I came down here prejudiced against all "colonies" but I wish now that I were a millionaire in order to make it more of what it is. MacDowell knew what he was about. Unfortunately it is absolutely necessary to be here in order to understand what it means. One summer of it in one of the isolated studios, with an open wood fire, would undo you for life. You ought to be glad that you are married—and I have a suspicion that you are not sorry.

Write me a letter and tell me what is good for a fractured future. I have Moody's unpublished poems, but with a few exceptions they don't tell me very much. I doubt if Moody himself would have published more than half of them as they stand and I have dreaded to say so to Mrs. Moody and so make a bigger personal hit than ever. She has not yet sent me the first act of the "Eve" drama, which I fancy to be the real thing as far as it goes. If Torrence thinks me too severe with the other poems (they were sent to him at the same time) he may be right and I hope that I am wrong.—Of course this is confidential.

TO MRS. WILLIAM VAUGHN MOODY

Peterborough, August 27, 1911
I have taken the liberty to make a few comments in pencil on the margins of poems rather than bother you with a long letter. They are not of much value, as you will see, but they may possibly give you a few suggestions. After reading the poems and the first act of the drama [1] several times, I am still of the opinion that both poems and first act ought first to be published with the earlier books in one volume. It seems to me a five volume edition of poetry and prose might better be deferred for a few years. But of course in the long run it will make no difference how Will's work is brought out. It will find its place and keep it in spite of anything his friends may or may not do.

I have little to say in the way of criticism that I have not said in marginal notes already referred to. "A Prairie Ride" still seems to me to be an unfinished experience, not worthy of a place with the other poems and I am a little in doubt as to the value of "The Fountain," though I should not think of suggesting its omission. I may be wrong about "slothful" in "I Am the Woman," but it seems to me to be a false note. Of course there is no need of my calling your attention to the obvious mistake in "A Second Coming" (maze).

This poem, "Old Pourquoi," and "I Am the Woman" are perhaps the best, though nearly all of them are stamped with genius as with a signature. I thank you most sincerely for letting me see them, and I feel that I should apologize for not having been in a hurry to let them go. If I can be of any kind of service, I am sure that you will let me know.

[Postscript]
I should not think of omitting the passage in "Eve" beginning with "The first that I remember," etc. But I must say that the other passage, on jealousy, does not appeal to me, either as being in place or of much importance. This act as a whole, however, is magnificent. It leaves me with a maddening sense of disappointment that the others should have to remain unwritten. I hope that the two-volume suggestion may commend itself to you (one of poetry and one of prose) but very likely it will not.

Peterborough, Sunday
[Envelope dated September 18, 1912]

... I have packed my play off to the typewriter and ought to have it in a few days; and here, I regret to say, comes the sad part of my letter. I don't want to make you restless or uncomfortable for I know that your building expenses must be pulling heavily on you; but having gone as far as I have into the playwriting game I can't stop now with the novels behind me (at any rate I would write the damned things), and poetry is so far in the future as to its tail that I can't reach it yet with any kind of salt and economy. In regard to the plays I know that there is only one thing for me to do. I don't ask you to share John Blair's enthusiasm, for the present at any rate, but there is no harm in my saying that he will do everything that he can for me with managers, and he knows nearly all of them, and if this finds you in a position to gamble a little more on my future, I can only offer in return the one security at my command—and that is that I shall do everything in my power to make good. If you find that you can't you will say so, and you need have no fear of my not understanding you. For the typewriting and the other absolutely necessary expenses I must make a raise from some source or other for I am high and dry—or shall be in a few days, and—oh, well, you understand what that means without my going any further into details.

I am about ready to begin work on a new comedy and hope to have the scaffolding all up by the time I reach New York. I go from here (in about a week) to Plainfield, to stay a while with Mrs. Davidge [1] and "Uncle Harry" [2] and then to Cornwall for another visitation upon the Ledoux. When your shack is ready I shall be glad to inspect it and to suggest any improvements that may present themselves to my articulate brain—always assuming, of course, that you are still willing to receive me. By way of recommendation I will say that I have lately acquired several new symptoms of sanity and that I am feeling better than I have felt at any time during the past ten or twelve years. If ever I get out of my infernal state of hitherto chronic indigence I shall sing songs from housetops and probably be arrested, though I shall be entirely sober. The demon highball is far behind me, but I do not look back upon him unkindly. On the contrary, I don't know just how I should have got through the "Valley of the Shadow" without him. You may call your Chasm a Valley, if you like, but I shall still reserve my likes to a Valley of my own which will be very queer, and rather long, and will have a tendency to make people sit up, if it is done as it should be done. It is in the distance now, but I know it is there for I can see it. It will be as cheerful as hell (which it is, or was) and there will be a foggy sunrise at the end with the fog gradually disappearing from a land of joy and song and grasshoppers.

Please let me hear from you at once and pardon my reminding you that I can't have my play until I can pay the typewriter. It's a great and terrible world.

TO LOUIS V. LEDOUX

63 West 83d Street, New York
[Postmarked Oct. 1, 1912]
I'm sorry to write to you on half a sheet of paper after all the good things you have been saying about me in the *Times,* but my case is imperative as I have two notes to write and only one sheet left. There is more paper outside,

but I am too lazy just now to go out and get it.—I wish to
thank you all through for your *Times* letter, which is from
its point of attack altogether the best thing that I have
yet read about my *Town*. I make this qualification, not
wishing to agree too eagerly with your praise, as such.
The publication of such intelligent criticism of what my
books are supposed at least to signify gives me a great deal
of pleasure at a time when I need a little cheering up. The
woes of the wagon are many and great, but its rewards
are said to be considerable, and I have an eye out for them
along the roadside. After a year or so of riding, I'll tell you
more about it, and you will not understand a damned word,
and then you will be fortunate. I understand that you are
fishing somewhere in Canada. When you get back let me
know your plans for the rest of the month. I shall be at
this address until the end of this week and perhaps longer.
If you are back by that time I can run—or rather ride—up
to see you.

Blair tells me that my play will act, but he doesn't like
the people in it very much. I don't think he is more than
half-right in his interpretation of them, but I am hardly in
a position to say much. He is going to give the thing to a
manager as soon as I have reduced the first act to less
formidable proportions. I think of calling my next play
"The Scrap-Heap"—but now it seems to me that I should
not in the nature of things live to finish it. How do you like
"The Dewdrop" instead? I don't think it has ever been
used.

With best wishes to you and your lady

I am

Yours respectfully

La Tourette
Richmond, Staten Island
23 February, 1913

Your letter found me after much travelling and I was glad to find out where it was that you were concealing yourself. And that I was correct in assuming that you sent the copy of *Kim* that I received in Peterborough.

I gather from your letter that you are fairly well contented in Brazil and with your Portuguese poets, who are, I regret to say, as unknown to me as I am to them. My knowledge of that literature is confined to what I don't know about Camoens; and therefore I envy your privilege of breaking into an entirely new poetic country. Being otherwise rational and normal as you are, you are mighty lucky in having a corner for poetry in your nature, and you ought to sing songs of thanksgiving to the rising sun that you are not one of the poor devils who have to make the stuff. I suppose you do make more or less of it, but you don't show the effects of your dissipation on the outside.

Please don't ask me anything more about my novels, or too much about my plays. The novels are extinct; and when I have satisfied myself and all my friends that I cannot write a play, I shall probably have the good sense to go back to poetry. The chief objection I have to poetry—after forty—is that it has a way of making Bellevue or Blackwell's Island appear unpleasantly democratic and adjacent. I see no immediate prospect of entertainment in either place, however, and I may be going to make a fortune. I don't like to think of where I should be now if it had not been for your astonishing father. He fished me out of hell by the hair of the head, and so enabled me to get my last book together, and in all probability to get it published. I hope sincerely that I have made him understand that I know this.

. . . I went down to Oyster Bay not long ago with Percy MacKaye and ran into Captain Amundsen and President Finley going in the same direction. It was a good day and I am very sorry that you were not there.

TO LEWIS M. ISAACS

La Tourette, March 7, 1913

You and Mrs. Isaacs wished to know what Ames [1] would have to say about *The Porcupine,* and I needn't be long in telling you. He professes to like it immensely himself but thinks it would pass over the heads of an audience and leave them wondering what it was all about. He may be right; I don't pretend to know.—Anyhow, I'm glad to say that I see signs of an early deliverance from my literary gallivanting for the past three years and a prospect of getting down to poetry again. It's a hard lot, but it seems to be the only thing that I can do and at the same time have any clear notion of what I am doing. I have finished the other play—*Van Zorn*—and shall give it to the typewriter tomorrow. When it is copied I'll bring it over and let you read it—if your courage holds out.

TO JOHN HAYS GARDINER

La Tourette, March 9, 1913

Thank you for the *Post* article, which I had not seen. It is a bit sad that it should have come at just this time, for I have lately made up my mind to do as I told you one evening at the Harvard Club that I ought to do, and would do if I were a little bigger man. I don't know whether I am a bigger man or not, but I do know that I shall never make any money by writing plays, and probably not in any other way. It isn't that I can't write a play, so far as the technique goes—in fact, I believe it is admitted that I can—but I cannot hit the popular chord, and for the simple reason that there is no immediately popular impulse in *me*. In poetry this is an advantage, but for commercial playwriting it is deadly. When I come down out of myself and try to write for the crowd, I perpetrate the damnedest rubbish that you ever heard of, and I seem to have no guiding hand to let me know what I am doing. I see now that my past three years of floundering in prose have been due to nothing more serious than the fact that I had temporarily written myself out. At last I can see light again, and I am going to write another book of poems; and then I shall know to some extent what I am about. I hope I haven't "got into" you enough to make you feel dissatisfied with my change of plans. I am pretty confident that you will be glad in the end.

I enclose a letter from Ames about *The Porcupine*. I think he is right, and I feel sure that he will say pretty much the same about the new play that I have just sent to the typewriter. I thought some time ago that I had other plays in sight, but I can see now that they are not only far off, but gradually dissolving into nothing. To be candid, I must say that I'm glad of it. I don't believe the human brain was ever constructed that could stand much more of the kind of wear and tear of conflicting activities than mine has undergone during the past three years, and I am sure that mine could not stand much more of it.

I feel that I have given the thing a fair trial and that it would be unfair to you as well as to myself to waste any more of my life in doing something for which I have come to see that I am not fitted.

I haven't seen Noyes'[1] book, but I hope to get hold of it. Please send me a word and let me know how my reversion to type strikes you.

TO HERMANN HAGEDORN

129 West 83rd Street, New York City
December 15, 1913

I'm sorry to talk about cheques with you again, and so I won't—except to tell you that this one came like manna. If I weren't writing a book that I believe in, I should feel like sending your twenty-five back and trying to sell peanuts, only I know I couldn't sell them. But we'll talk, as you say, about this later, when I see you. Perhaps the best thing for me to do would be to leave here the morning before Christmas and to stay over a day or two. I feel that I ought to make every day count this winter; and I know that I shall have too good a time (although I may not show it) to do any work at your place. I shall loaf for a day or two and do as little damage as possible.

If you tried to find any kind of hero in Levi,[1] I don't wonder that you didn't succeed in caring much for him. He is just a poor devil, totally miscast, and with not much in his head anyhow. The world is peppered with his kind, and I simply drew his picture to let people see what they thought about it in the light of contemporary materialism. If materialism is true, then parenthood is assuredly the greatest of all crimes, and the sooner the much advertised "race" is annihilated, the better. But you know my own opinions, and therefore you know that I'm not a materialist. As a matter of fact, I suppose I'm the damnedest optimist that ever lived. Let me know if my plan for Christmas will be agreeable.

TO MRS. LIONEL S. MARKS
(*Josephine Preston Peabody*)

129 West 83rd Street
February 3, 1914

I don't mean to be egotistic, but at the same time I don't believe there is anyone on earth who can tell me, since the publication of my last two books, anything about the chills and silences that appertain to the poetry business. For two years after the appearance of each of them, there was hardly as much as a patter of intelligent appreciation. Therefore I think it is too early for you to say jug-jug and tereu-tereu over the *Wolf*.[1] If your experience has been anything like mine, you may, with more or less reason, look for two or three signs in the critical sky sometime about next April or May. The one perfunctory skimming that a book of verse gets from the rank and file of reviewers is in most cases worse than nothing—as you must know by experience, since you have written books that are worth while.

I liked the *Wolf* because I liked it, not because it gave me "bread". The world doesn't want bread from poets, unless it is so completely disguised that they mistake it for cake; and while great poetry has nearly always an ethical value, history would seem to indicate that Apollo doesn't care a d-damn for the Uplift. You have done your best work when you have forgotten what a rotten place this world is. You needn't ever worry about the ethical presence in your own stuff, for there will always be rather too much than too little of it. And if this has a queer sound, coming as it does from such an incurable preacher as I am—why, then, be sorry for me, and don't write any more *Singing Men*. If you will give the next three or four years to the getting together of a small book containing the best elements of your first two, and *The Singing Leaves,* and the *Little Past*—avoiding all hifalutin diction, and more or less nebulous generalizing about an entirely hypothetical human that has never existed and probably never will exist, you will be a happy woman again, and incidentally (though of course this is not so important) a more valuable wife and mother. God forgive me, meanwhile, and all the bad jokes that I have ever made in all my letters. Fortunately, most of them have never been read. "People don't do such things"—to quote the immortal words of Assessor Brack in *Hedda Gabler,* and as a rule I don't write 'em any more. But I'm writing this one to you because I likes you werry much and don't want you to consume yourself in trying to reform the world. I don't mean to be discouraging, but you can't do it. If you must insist upon destroying yourself in the attempt, however, there are more painless ways available than that of poetry.

I'm not going to read this over, for if I do I know I shall not send it. And if I don't send this one, the good gods and little devils only know when I shall write another.—I'm glad that you are "Knowing Yourself." I've been trying to do something of the kind for forty years.

TO MRS. LOUIS V. LEDOUX

129 West 83d Street
April 23, 1914

I suppose you would be pretty considerably surprised if I were to tell you that I'm going to be married. Well, I'm not going to be, and so you won't have to be surprised. No doubt you will say it's a mean trick on my part to scare a lady when she is away on a journey, but I wanted to say something funny, and that was the funniest thing I could think of with my poor brain in its present state of continued vacuity, and you will have to make the most of it. I have recently finished a poem which I may possibly sell to somebody for five dollars—if it happens to come to them after a good dinner—and I'm getting ready to work on another which will probably keep me out of jail for the next five or six weeks. It's a thing that I have had with me for a long time, and one that I wish to get rid of before it becomes a habit.—Nothing whatever has happened to me since you and Louis went away except that I have been rather lonesome without your place to go to. I go to other places, but somehow I have never succeeded in acquiring with other people the same sense of freedom, security, rapport, expression, and general well-being that I begin to feel as soon as I inflict myself upon you and yours for better or worse. You needn't let this frighten you, like my opening words— which were as playful as an elephant with a jew's-harp —for I'm going to give you both a long rest. I'll be getting out of this town before you get back, and my solemn countenance will not appear in your view again until I shall know whether or not I'm to have another book done by New Year's Eve. If I don't I shan't worry, but I have had a sort of fool notion that I might if I kept myself busy. There is no earthly reason why I should, for I'm sure that I never dreamed of doing anything of the kind before. If I succeed, I shall very likely be sorry and be served right for putting on so many industrious airs, when I know, inside, that I'm the laziest thing that ever looked at Percy MacKaye through a mental spyglass. Apart from his infernally humiliating activity, he seems to have acquired among other accomplishments the art of living and getting fat without the aid of food or sleep. He eats an apple or a peanut now and then, when he can think of absolutely nothing else to do, goes to bed sometime in the morning if he thinks it worth while, and gets up at about the time when I'm beginning to get some sleep. I have studied him, and I have tried to follow his example and take myself seriously—but I can't do it. I tried it the other evening after dinner and the effect made me laugh. Then I went to the Winter Garden, and that made me cry. Then I came home and read H. G. Wells's latest false prophecy, *The World Set Free,* until three o'clock and finally went to sleep. I got up at half-past ten, ate a hearty breakfast like a man going to be hanged, and then felt surprisingly well—so well that I walked twenty blocks and then came home and finished the poem that I think I may sell for five dollars. I'm almost sorry that I'm not going to be married, for I'm sure, in that case, you'd find this letter interesting.

TO MRS. LOUIS V. LEDOUX

Peterborough, August 10, 1914
I had begun to wonder what had become of you and Louis when your letter came to let me know. Ever since then it has been staring up at me from the top of my badly littered table as if to let me know, in addition, that I have lost all sense of epistolary decency. I'm beginning to fear that I'm incurable on this point. I think it strange and altogether wrong if my friends don't write to me, and the mere fact that I never write to them doesn't seem to make any difference. But, as I have said before, I have never succeeded in understanding why I have any friends, or why I should have any, considering my specialized way of treating them.

It seems to me that your sister has more than one person's share of trouble. I hope, at any rate, that she is all right again by this time and that her numerous fights with events will not result in making her altogether a believer in an almighty devil. He isn't almighty, but he's pretty near it. He knows his limitations, and that knowledge makes him mad, and accordingly he makes this world as good an imitation of hell as he can; and at this moment his possibilities appear to be considerable.

I don't seem to have much to say about myself. I'm pegging away on the new book and admiring the cover of *Van Zorn*—wondering whether or not I can live up to it. If you don't like it, I shall never have anything more to say to you —though you may find as much fault as you like with what is inside of it. *C. C.* is to be brought out in the same style, and other things, I fancy, if what little brain I have left doesn't dry up entirely. I have written a poem about Rum, and another about Washington Square. . . . I am altogether better natured and more reasonable than I was during my last month in New York, when Dr. Ledoux[1] must have thought, with good cause, that I was going to pieces. I have had three or four periods when I seemed to be going, but somehow I haven't yet quite gone. I may go when the critics get after the two books of mine that are soon to come out, though I'm glad to say that such a thing is not likely. Something less tangible than being jumped on will be likely to settle my affairs.

Please ask Louis to write me a letter and to give me some kind of account of himself. I still see him pouring poison into the porches of the Mutt's[2] left ear, but I hope my vision is not true.

Peterborough, June 26, 1915

The Mutt is a bitter disappointment to me. In fact, I can't see any good in him at all, and I don't believe there is any. I shouldn't even call him a gentleman; and yet he seemed to be well born, and I know that he has had a good bringing up. On the whole, his case is rather a sad one.—To leave an unpleasant subject, let me say that I was very glad, though not necessarily surprised, to hear about Mackail's letter. My only surprise is that which one has to feel when he knows that an Englishman has read a book of American verse. I am sure that "Persephone," when Louis gets it printed, will attract a great deal of attention among the small band of the faithful (meaning Mackail and his like) and I am equally sure that it will not please Miss Harriet Monroe. . . . I'm glad anyhow that you saw the *Pirates*. I've forgotten pretty much all of it except the Policemen's Chorus —tarantara—which I like better, in some ways, than the last act of *Prometheus Unbound,* which somehow doesn't quite come off. This makes me think of a friend of Isaacs' who sat behind X on a Fifth Avenue bus and saw this marginal note in a copy of Keats that he (X) was reading: "Neat, but not as I should have done it." . . . Of course you won't read all this, but you will see, at any rate, that I have written a longer letter to you than I have written to anybody since I was a small boy. The R. T.'s are quiet and apparently thriving. This morning we had a hail storm, and I read *The Valley of Fear*[1] but was disappointed.

TO KERMIT ROOSEVELT

Peterborough, June 28, 1915

Thank you for your letter and for your pleasant words about *Van Zorn,* which seems to be giving trouble to several otherwise worthy people. It remains to be seen whether it is simply a failure, or whether it is so different from most plays in subject matter and construction that some time will be required for its assimilation. In the meantime, I can only consider it in the light of Otto's Farewell,[1] which you are good enough to like. I shall have another play of a very different nature for you in September [2], and a new book of poems in February.[3] After that I may be decoyed by the devil into writing a long thing of about three thousand lines—not quite so free and easy and experimental as *Captain Craig,* in which many can see no manner of good. This is rather unfortunate, for it serves as a dead weight on the rest of the book. But time will attend to all that, if there is anything to attend to. . . .

TO MRS. LOUIS V. LEDOUX

Peterborough, August 30, 1915

If you could know how many times I have intended to acknowledge your last letter I am sure you would be entirely satisfied; and this applies as well to Louis. Please assure him that I did not sic the erratic French on him; and add that I was rather annoyed to learn that he had made his appearance. He seems to have a paranoiac determination to label all my characters and his identification of Louis with *Van Zorn* is a fair specimen of his acumen in that direction. —I have written one thing of about 300 lines since I left

New York, and to save my 15-½ neck I cannot do anything
else that gives me any kind of satisfaction. It is a good thing
for me that what I have will make a fair-sized book—
though I'm sure that two or three more things will produce
themselves before the fire in Louis' den—that is, if he doesn't
"disinvite" me in the meantime. I have a little more than
half-decided to try Boston this winter, but I shall very
likely give in as soon as I get a sniff of Forty-second Street
and a sight of Broadway. It's a bad thing to be poisoned. I
am told the Ben Jonson is coming out in the *Drama
Quarterly*, but I have nothing official—least of all a cheque.
On the whole, I think I'm pretty well, but as I grow older
I get madder and madder with myself when I'm not producing something. I don't suppose it really makes a damn bit
of difference whether I produce anything or not, so long as
I'm such an exemplary character.

Yours, with great regard,
JOHN B. GOUGH

TO AMY LOWELL

66 West 83rd Street,
26 November, 1915

Once in a while—not very often—it happens that a thing
one really wants comes unexpectedly into his possession.
"So has it fallen here". Your big book on *Six French Poets*
came to me the other day and I got myself immediately into
a rocking-chair, after the manner of Stéphane Mallarmé
and read the thing halfway through before I found out what
time it was. You have surely done a good service to the
poets and to the public. I could have known, or assumed,
your equipment for such a piece of work, but I could not
have been sure, without evidence, of your infernal industry.

Having now read all that you have written, and much of what you have quoted, I beg to thank you in all sincerity for writing the book and for being good enough to send me a copy. I doubt if any copy will fall into more appreciative hands.

For myself I am thinking over some new performances which may or may not occur. When I do this I sit for the most part in a rocking-chair—"rocking, in fact," though not violently. I hope that M. Mallarmé's classic sanction of the abhorred practice will keep you from striking me from your list of friends. William Cowper (whom I fancy you read every day) did not include the offence in his list of evils that make a man a creature not to be known. I formed the habit when I was a small child—when I used to rock myself in a chair many sizes too large for me and wonder why the deuce I should ever have been born. I was indignant about it for several years, but I've got all over that—though I may not have answered my own question in all ways to my satisfaction. The Macmillan printers are now at work on my latest intimations of mortality, which I hope will interest you a little.

TO HERMANN HAGEDORN

66 West 83rd Street,
December 6, 1915

. . . As for your superlatives in regard to my own efforts, please accept again my sincerest thanks, but quietly remember that I have never encouraged the use of such epithets. . . . I hope this doesn't sound ungrateful, for God knows how grateful I am to you for your encouragements. I wish merely to have you and a few others understand that I have never had any top-lofty notions as to the security of my alleged appointed seat among those of the western poets, which aren't so damned high—for the most part.

TO MRS. WILLIAM VAUGHN MOODY

66 West 83rd Street
December 10, 1915

I find it difficult to refuse you anything, but there are three or four good reasons why I do not feel that I could write anything worth while for the occasion you describe. I am up to my eyes in my new book. What room there is left over in my not very large brain is full of other work that I wish to get to as soon as possible, and furthermore I am not good at the kind of thing you want. However much or little my poetry may be worth, somehow prose is not my natural form of expression. I have to hammer and dig and sweat and swear and throw away and do over again ad infinitum even the smallest kind of serious article; and my experience has been such as to make me determined never to do anything of the kind again if there is any way out of it. I couldn't have written the *Fire-Bringer*, but I can understand how Will could have done it. But I shall never understand how the deuce he wrote his *History of English Literature*.[1] I should have worked six months over the first chapter and then thrown it away.

Last of all, the whole scheme of your evening doesn't appeal to me. It seems to me that we poor devils who are condemned to write poetry should write it, and not talk about it. Your plan seems to me to savor too much of mutual admiration, though of course I know that such a thought never entered your head. If I were to write about anybody, it would be about Will, who is more living than most of us— but what good would that do? His place is perfectly secure, and in the proper order of things, and through a proper perspective of years, the authoritative right words will be said for a public that will not have to be distrustful of contemporary praise—which doesn't amount to much except for the pleasure it gives to the living. Excuse me for wandering entirely away from the subject. Be sure to let me know when you come to town.

TO MRS. LOUIS V. LEDOUX

66 West 83rd Street,
December 10, 1915

Let me thank you for sending a bit of color into my morning, even though your remembrance is a bit suggestive of my own funeral. But things are not so bad as that. My nerves are just a little out of tune, like your small piano, and I'm doing what I can to set them right. I have no fault to find with the world, though it might seem, to the superficial observer, to be in a bad way just now. My trouble dates back some forty years, when I realized, at the age of five, that I was never going to be able to elbow my way to the Trough of Life. But I shall get over this attack, as I have got over others, and by the end of the day after Christmas I shall probably be dancing all over the city. . . .

TO DR. ALBERT R. LEDOUX

66 West 83d Street
March 2, 1916

It gave me great pleasure to recognize your handwriting when I came in last evening, and I hope you will observe that I record this pleasure as one that was felt before I knew what was in your letter. Schopenhauer says somewhere that we can always tell how much we care for a person by the sight of a letter from him or her, and my experience tells me that there is a great deal of truth in what he says. I wish I had his effective way of putting things at my command in order that I might say something at least partly adequate for your great kindness, wholly unexpected, at a time when it takes away a rather troublesome load of uncertainty that has been with me for some time past; for while I was not in any immediate difficulty, I was still near enough to difficulty to feel its pressure around the corner. And your surprising remembrance was all the more gratifying to me in view of the fact that I had begun to fancy that you might, and with good reason, have begun to be a little out of patience with the intermittent and more or less uncertain nature of my not very voluminous achievements. I always have the blues when I'm not producing something; and this is probably my logical punishment for wasting, or seeming to have wasted, so much time in the past. It may be fortunate for me that there is no way of measuring these things—but I do not consider it in any way fortunate that I cannot tell you how grateful I am for this new proof of your faith in what I am trying to do. I can only thank you once more, trusting that you will supply for yourself the substance of what I do not say in words.

What you say of the book [1] gives me, of course, another great pleasure. You are entirely right in assuming that the title poem is not a dirge. My purpose was to cheer people up and incidentally to indicate the futility of materialism as a thing to live by—even assuming the possible monstrous negation of having to die by it. Fortunately, again, it is a part of our destiny that we do not spend much of our time in wondering over these matters.

TO AMY LOWELL

66 West 83d Street
March 18, 1916

Let me thank you for your good words about my book and especially for your praise of "Ben Jonson," which several others have apparently succeeded in liking. But I must hasten to correct, or try to correct, what seems to be a false impression on your part in regard to the last poem in the book. Nothing could have been farther from my mind when I wrote "The Man" than any emissary of gloom or of despair. In the closing pages I meant merely, through what I supposed to be an obviously ironic medium, to carry materialism to its logical end and to indicate its futility as an explanation or a justification of existence. Perhaps you will read the poem again sometime and observe my "lesson" in the last line. I thought of printing it in italics, but changed my mind since I don't like 'em. I was sorry not to be able to attend the Grand Pierian Dinner at the Astor, but I realized at the eleventh hour that I was not fit. . . . Incidentally, and possibly in the hope of giving pain, I find it necessary to remind you now that what seems to me to be the very best of your *vers libre* is almost exclusively "human" in its subject matter, and therefore substantially old-fashioned. One reason why I haven't more to say on the subject is that I have absolutely no theories. I don't care a pinfeather what form a poem is written in so long as it makes me sit up. "Imagiste" work, *per se*, taken as a theory apart from one special form, seems to me rather too self-conscious and exclusive to stand the test of time. I feel pretty confident that if you had to sacrifice one or the other you would retain that part of your poetry that has in it the good and bad solid old-fashioned human qualities that make us all one crazy family of children, throwing things at each other across the table, and making faces at each other in *saecula saeculorum.*

TO HERMANN HAGEDORN

Peterborough, June 1, 1916

The ——s arrived here yesterday. Apparently as happy as two sparrows, which event makes me wonder if I was not a bit premature in my cloudy prognostications. At any rate I hope I was. I'm glad he is here, for in some strange way he has a stimulating effect on my sluggish creative faculties. I came here a week ago, and by way of getting "oiled up" I wrote a more or less dramatic poem [1] of 250 lines in three days. I haven't read it over yet, and so don't know what it is like; but I have at least the satisfaction of having achieved something, if only for my admirable fireplace.

. . . Life has taken on new color since my arrival at this place, and I am beginning really to believe that I am going to do something this summer. I remember that last evening with you with a special kind of pleasure. The combination of your company, *The Tempest,* and the clams, was a rare one.

TO HERMANN HAGEDORN

Peterborough, June 11, 1916

I don't suppose that I meant my remark about the sparrows to be taken too literally, but I'm glad to say that there do seem to be signs of something like a readjustment. The man-sparrow is still nervous and rotten, but nothing like so bad as he was last winter. The lady-sparrow seems to have had a jolt, or something; for she seems most subdued and miserable. Of course it may be only acting on her part, and she still may make the feathers fly as they never flew before. I can only hope that she won't. If she can keep herself together for another year or two, she may learn something.

I am most interested in H———'s play, and I'm glad to know that T. R. has got hold of him, and vice versa. They ought to have some fun together—H. being everything that I am not, in a humanly possible way. T. R. likes my book, but I see now that I never gave him an opportunity to make much out of me—even assuming that there is much, or anything, to be made. I fear that I am coming more and more to look upon myself as a more or less talented armadillo, and one that has spent much of its earlier existence in rolling down hill. Just now the animal is sunning itself on the top of a small knoll—or would be doing so if there were any sun in Peterborough.

I'm writing at a most immoral rate, but I don't yet know what I am writing, or who is going to read it. . . .

TO ARTHUR NEVIN

Peterborough, July 15, 1916

I find it rather difficult to say anything tangible or satisfactory about the relation of music and poetry—music being poetry, and poetry being music. Not long ago I attempted, in a newspaper interview, to define poetry as "a language that tells us, through a more or less emotional reaction, something that cannot be said." This might be an equally good, or bad, definition of music, but for the fact that the reader would balk instinctively at the qualifying "more or less" before "emotional"—the emotional reaction in the case of music that endures being unquestionably "more." And this, no doubt, is equally true of much of the best poetry, although it seems to me that words, in their very nature, no matter how intense or lyrical their expression, must obviously admit of subtleties of sound and sense that would not be possible in any conceivable combination of tones. As a layman, I cannot resist this opportunity to make myself offensive by setting down my by no means original belief that most of the present-day composers are carefully insuring oblivion for their names and their notes by forcing tones to do the work of words. On the other hand, it is equally true that many poets—Swinburne and Lanier, for example—have gone altogether too far in trying to make words do the work of tones. Generally speaking, I should be inclined to say that the field of poetry is infinitely more various and less definable than that of music, for the simple reason that poetry is language and music at the same time. There is no such thing as "programme" poetry, and some of us are almost willing to wish there might be no more "programme" music. Poetry has been called for centuries the greatest of the arts, but I should rather say that music and poetry are two—or rather three—manifestations of the greatest of the arts. At any rate this arrangement would leave the musician happy with a right to say that music (meaning tone) begins where poetry (meaning language) leaves off. But the tones of music will have to go faster and farther than they have yet gone if they expect or hope to keep the overtones of language far behind them.

TO MRS. LOUIS V. LEDOUX

Peterborough, July 30, 1916

I hope your party fulfilled all the requirements of such a business, whatever they are. My notion of a party is generally something to stay away from, though sometimes I

like to hear about them afterwards—that is, if anything
went wrong. I haven't any brain nowadays, and I know you
will pardon me if I don't send you a letter in reply to yours.
I've written 2200 lines of *Merlin*, and the darned thing is
still going. If I'm not locked up in some endowed institution
before the middle of August, I hope to have the thing done
by then. When I have spent a month or so in rewriting, it
will be as good and as bad as I'm likely to make it. Louis
tells me that he has sent his book to Brett [1], who will, I trust
and believe, see a way to publish it in spite of the high price
of paper. I am far from sure that he will publish my 2600
lines of *Merlin* when they are ready, but I shall be rather in
a mess if he doesn't. The thing seems to me to be interesting and, on the whole, entirely moral. It all depends on the
point of view. You may still call me an evangelist of ruin
when you have read it but you mustn't forget the redemp-
tion—even if you don't see it.

TO MRS. LOUIS V. LEDOUX

Peterborough, August 14, 1916
   I'm sorry you lost your party the other evening, but
otherwise I'm glad it rained, for probably you wouldn't have
written to me if it hadn't. I did not know before of Alan
Seeger's death. On the whole I think it was the best thing
for him, for I don't believe that he would ever have come
anywhere near to fitting himself into this interesting but
sometimes unfittable world. I haven't made a great success
in that way myself, as you and one or two others may have
begun by this time to suspect. In the meantime I can only
take off my hat to Seeger. He did the thing thoroughly, and
that is always something, if not everything.—Of course I
am mighty glad to hear about Louis' book, although I should
have been much surprised to hear anything different. Tell

him to write me a letter sometime when his powerful mind has no better occupation for its engine. . . . I have finished *Merlin,* after a fashion, and my unreliable nerves are paying for him to a certain extent. Nothing like what I had last winter, when I was doing nothing, and felt as if everything were skew-geed (only I knew it wasn't), but still a queer sort of premonition that I had better slow up for a while. I hope to rewrite a good part of it before I leave here, but if I don't I shan't worry much. Even for a lazy man, I think I've done a pretty fair nine weeks' work, having written much of the thing twice. But I'd better stop bragging about myself, or you will say that my six-cylinder New England conscience is carrying me back into my industrious and illustrious past, when I used to see two or three years go by without my doing a dim thing to justify my existence— although I can see now that some things were being done for me—even in the subway, which still makes me sick when I think of it. The editors of *The Seven Arts* are still fighting—so Miss Lowell tells me—over my dialogue between two sisters, which I wrote when I came here last May. I don't see what there is in it to fight about, but I rather expect, all the same, to get it back. This is a day to make Dionysus forget to drink, but we haven't had many like it. Please don't misinterpret this, for I haven't had one since the middle of May, and haven't wanted one. I had a few in Boston, chiefly because I was in Boston. I don't believe that I shall ever try to live there for thirty days again.

On the whole I'm pretty frisky, and Mrs. Perry [1] is painting my picture in Hancock on Sundays.

[Postscript]
By the way, can Louis get Gilbert Murray's address for me sometime when he is in town? Anytime within two or three weeks.

TO AMY LOWELL

66 West 83rd Street
October 31, 1916
The general effect of your new book is something, I fancy,
like that of an avalanche. I haven't yet quite recovered
from the surprises and the bruises, but I am glad for the experience, for I know more now about the powers that are
lying in wait for me than I knew before your book came.
Whether this kind of effect is the ultimate mission of art I
am not prepared to say, but you may be interested to know
that you have given me a pretty good shaking up; and I
am not, I believe, very easily shaken. Somehow I think that
you will not consider me far out of the way when I tell you
that I have had the most pleasure and the least qualified
satisfaction from "Patterns," "The Cross Roads," "1777,"
"Bronze Tablets" (all four). Then "Bombardment," "Nightmare," and the last section, "Towns in Colours." This list
is, of course rather arbitrary, and it is one that may easily
be modified or enlarged. . . .

TO ROBERT FROST

66 West 83rd Street
February 2, 1917
Let me thank for your book, which came to me the other
day by way of the Macmillans. I don't know how long they
have had it, but I do know that they are sinners in such
matters.
In "Snow," "In the Home Stretch," "Birches," "The Hill
Wife," and "The Road Not Taken" you seem undoubtedly
to have added something permanent to the world, and I

must congratulate you. I like everything else in the book, but these poems seem to me to stand out from the rest; and I fancy somehow that you will not wholly disagree with me. Please give my best regards to Mr. Young and believe me

Yours always, sincerely

E. A. Robinson

TO MRS. LIONEL S. MARKS
(Josephine Preston Peabody)

66 West 83rd St.,
March 31, 1917

Thank you for your good wishes. I needed them. The thing is given under the worst imaginable conditions, but those who see it sit through it and appear to be interested, and possibly a little bewildered. At any rate I have the satisfaction of knowing that I wasn't an ass in believing it would act. It comes out just as I saw it in my mind's eye—only a little more so. It isn't a bad show, but I doubt if there will ever be much of a public for it.

Yours sincerely,

R. CRUSOE

TO LEWIS M. ISAACS

Peterborough, June 3, 1917

In spite of about the worst weather I have ever lived through, I have contrived somehow to write five hundred lines of *Lancelot* in eight days. I knew something would have to happen after the winter that I went through, and that was the reason why I was so anxious to get through it. I suppose all this goes back to the old saying that every-

thing has to be paid for, especially by those who live outside the hive. Anyhow, I'm here; and I hope to stay here
for some time. If all goes well the book will be comfortably
done before I leave, although I don't expect or wish to keep
up the rate of speed at which I have started—really started,
I mean, for I find that I shall not use much of the fragmentary stuff that I sketched out in New York. As a matter
of fact the thing wasn't ripe then, and I shouldn't have
bothered with it but for the annoying feeling I had that I
ought to be doing something to justify my seemingly negative existence. It wasn't really negative, but I doubt if I
could make anyone believe that. . . . From now on I see
nothing for me but a righteous and orderly life, with a book
now and then to punctuate its harmless monotony, and then,
when I have earned it, a hole in the ground with whatever
may or may not come after. This is not a bad or an unpleasant programme, if I can carry it out.

I hope you are going to get down here sometime this
summer. Let me know what you plan and remember me to
all your admirable family. I have been trying, through the
foregoing, to tell you that I am just now in uncommonly
good spirits.

TO L. N. CHASE [1]

Peterborough, July 11, 1917
I find it rather difficult to answer your letter, much as I
appreciate it and your motive in writing it. I am handi-
capped at the start in having no biography and no theories.
You will find as much in Who's Who as I have to say about
myself personally; and as for my work, I have hoped that
it might speak—not very loudly, perhaps—for itself. Ten
years ago I was called a radical, and most readers looked
sideways at my work on account of its unconventional use

of so-called simple language. I suppose that I have always depended rather more on context than on vocabulary for my poetical effects, and this offense has laid me open to the charge of over-subtlety on the part of the initiated and of dullness on the part of the dull. Whatever merit my work may or may not possess, I fancy that it will always be a waste of time for any reader who has not a fairly well developed sense of humor—which, as someone has said before, is a very serious thing—to bother with it. When I tell you that my poem called "The Gift of God" (in *The Man Against the Sky*) has been interpreted as a touching tribute to our Saviour, you will require no further comment upon this point.

When I was younger, I was very much under the influence of Wordsworth and Kipling, but never at all, so far as I am aware, under that of Browning, as many seem to believe. As a matter of fact, I have never been able to understand the alleged resemblance unless it can be attributed to my use of rather more colloquial language than "poetic diction" has usually sanctioned. I began the writing of verse long before I was old enough to know better, and I fancy that I am safe in saying that my style, such as it is, was pretty well formed by the time my first book was published, in 1896.

As for my methods of work, there does not seem to be much for me to say. As a rule I see the end of a thing before I begin it (if I don't see it then, I am likely never to see it) and the rest of the process is simply a matter of how the thing goes. Sometimes it goes rapidly, sometimes slowly; and so far as I can see, one method produces about the same result as the other, provided I know what I am trying to say. When occasionally I have become disgusted and thrown an unfinished poem away, it has always been because I had really nothing to write about. I have written a sonnet in twenty minutes as a joke ("Another Dark Lady") and I have tinkered others ("The Clerks", for example) for a month. Generally speaking, I should be inclined to say that if some sort of first draft doesn't form itself rather quickly, the final product is likely to be unsatisfactory; but with something definite and worth while to work on, any amount of labor may justify itself. Again, it may not. I imagine, however, that the worst poetry in the world has been written in the finest frenzy of inspiration; and so, probably, has the best.

When you ask me to annotate individual poems, I find myself in another difficulty. While nearly everything that I have written has a certain amount of personal coloring, I do not recall anything of mine that is a direct transcription of experience. For example, I have never liked the sound of church-bells; and the sound of their ringing one evening for the wedding of two people in whom I had not the remotest interest brought about a mood in me that made me write "On the Night of a Friend's Wedding"—a sonnet, by the way, that was begun suddenly, and later worked over for an immoderate length of time. But I was younger then than I am now, and time didn't count.

I thought nothing when I was writing my first book of working for a week over a single line; and while I don't do it any more, I am sure that my technique is better for those early grilling exercises. In fact, I am now more than inclined to believe that the technical flabbiness of many writers is due to the lack in earlier years of just such grilling—in the years when one is not conscious of how hard he is working and of how much time he is wasting—unless he is ready to gamble his life away for the sake of winning the possible conjunction of a few inevitable words. It seems an odd stake to play for so heavily, and perhaps it is fortunate for the race that so few are playing for it. Of course almost everyone is writing verse nowadays, but not many are taking it seriously enough to let it interfere with their meal tickets.

I haven't my books at hand, but for poems to read aloud you might consider "John Evereldown," "The Tavern," "The Clerks," "Amaryllis" (*Children of the Night*); "Morgan and Fingal," "Cortège" (*Captain Craig*); "The Master," the "Calvary" poem, "Vickery's Mountain," from *The Town Down the River;* "Doctor of Billiards" (which, by the way, is not a plea for the suppression of vice); and whatever you like from *The Man Against the Sky*—"Flammonde" and "The Gift of God," perhaps. The end of "Master" might possibly give pleasure. . . .

The poems that I have cited do not seem to require any explanation—with the exception perhaps of "Vickery's Mountain," which is after all merely a study of human inertia, which is in Vickery's case something stronger than he is. Flammonde is the man who sees but cannot do for himself, "others he saved," etc. "John Evereldown" and "The Tavern" are purely fanciful sketches, without ethical or symbolical significance. "Doctor of Billiards" pictures a man who seems to be throwing away a life which, for some reason known only to himself, is no longer worth living. "The Man Against the Sky" is a protest against a material explanation of the universe. "Morgan and Fingal" is merely an episode with overtones.

TO LEWIS M. ISAACS

Peterborough, July 18, 1917
. . . I am still pegging away at *Lancelot,* which seems in a way of coming out six hundred lines longer than *Merlin.* I have about 2300 at present. I am glad that you feel as you do about these long poems and that you are not counting too much on immediate recognition. I was pretty sure that the free verse enthusiasts could not, or would not, see what

I was driving at, in *Merlin,* but as all the critics for whose opinions I have any respect—that is, as many of them as I have heard from—seem to have no difficulty with the poem, I am not worrying about it. I should like to write a Tristram, but owing to my precarious method (perhaps method isn't quite the word) of existence, I am not sure that I might not be on safer ground if I were to go to work on another book like the "Man". I shall know more about this when I have *Lancelot* off my hands. I have a notion that the publishers may be inclined to balk at a Tristram if not possibly at *Lancelot,* but I have lived long enough to realize that there is no use in worrying about trifles like that. I don't know just how *Merlin* has been going, but I fancy rather slowly. I was told just the other day that most of the so-called reviewers can make nothing of him and for that reason have dodged him. Most of those who have written anything at all have copied the publisher's notice on the jacket—and I supposed that the thing was as clear as daylight! Well, I still think so—even if I don't know what to think of the human brain. The editor of *Poetry* reads the Vivian part as owlishly as if it were an ultimatum to Germany, and refers rather naively to "Merlin's pompous love-making," while the poor devil thought all the time that he was amusing and perhaps a bit original. I hadn't heard of K. R.'s going to England, which seems rather surprising. When I left him in New York he was on his way to Plattsburg. Nevin is in good spirits over his two operas, and Mrs. MacDowell seems to be, for her, comparatively lively. The place would be better if you were here, but even if you are not here, it is good to know that you are somewhere. Give my best regards to Mrs. Isaacs and the children.

[Postscript]
I shall be glad to take advantage of your typewriting offer

if you are sure that it will not interfere with anything. But this will come later.

Peterborough, August 25, 1917

It was good to get your letter and to know that you have survived the summer. I haven't really known much about it, having been on my Camelot job for about eight hours a day. I'm now about half-way through the third and last writing of L. & G.[1] and I'm taking it fairly easy—in fact I can't take it any other way, considering what isn't left of me. I'm well enough, generally speaking, but my skull is a nut. Perhaps I'm not myself. Anyhow I've got the thing, and there are a little over 3400 lines of it. What its fate will be is more than I can say. All I can say is that it seems to me to be rather the best thing that I have done, if that means anything. . . . By the way, if you should happen to care to have the MS., I'll be very glad to give it to you. If you don't care for such lumber, I'll hand it over to Ledoux. Please let me know about this soon, in order to avoid any annoyance over a small matter.

I saw the notices of *Merlin*, which seems to have scared most of the so-called reviewers. At any rate, they have generally passed it by or copied the publisher's notice on the jacket. The whole reviewing business, if it were not a joke, would be lamentable. If a boy or a girl hasn't brains enough to do anything else, he or she is set to reviewing books. They might as well try to play the fiddle, and probably many of them do. I'll be glad to see you all again before long, but I can't yet say just when.

TO MRS. LOUIS V. LEDOUX

Peterborough, August 26, 1917

I can understand your feeling of insufficiency in wartime for I have the same feeling myself; only mine is worse, as I am a trousered animal and therefore more to be looked upon to do something noisy and adequate. I don't believe that you need worry very much.—I'm about half through the third writing of L. & G., and hope to send the whole thing off to the typewriter by the middle of September— in which event I ought to have it sometime in October for Louis to read, if he can stand it, before the fire in Cornwall. I think both of you are pretty long-suffering to ask again for my dismal visitation on your premises. I'm not so dismal inside, however, except when I am writing novels. I'm glad that I haven't got to write those novels again. As for the poem, I can only hope for the best. I don't know whether I deserve a crown or a foolscap for trying to make Guinevere interesting—a fact that hasn't to my knowledge been accomplished heretofore—but she must have had a way with her or there wouldn't have been such an everlasting amount of fuss made over her. Anyhow, I've got her, such as she is, and she is more or less in evidence to the extent of 3400 lines. I'm still wondering just what kind of face the publishers are going to make when I take the thing in to them.

If it should be entirely convenient to you and Louis I fancy that I am likely to come in on you about the middle of October. You might let me know when you get back from your travels.

TO RENÉE LEDOUX
(Aged nine)

[Postmarked Boston]
June 12, 1918

I know this is not the right kind of paper for a man to
use when writing to a lady, but I know several things that
nobody would ever suspect. You may not know this; but
your father does. He knows such things because he has a
great mind. You tell your father that he has a great mind
and he will give you another penny to put in your purse,
and he may give you his green pencil. Did you ever have
an English Sparrow fly up to your window and cling to the
screen and look at you as if he liked you? One did that for
me this morning. But I forgot. He couldn't do it for you, because you have no screens. That is why you have so many
bugs—I mean insects—and reptiles and ornithorhynchuses
in your house during the warm weather. They scare your
mother, but still she loves them. She pretends that she
doesn't. I am so glad to know that the big old cow is the
little calf's father and that you have a black pig. The other
evening I went to a Pop Concert and heard the fiddlers
play "The March of the Little Lead Soldiers," and somehow
it made me think of *you*. I hope you will hear it sometime
yourself, and I hope it will make you think of *me*. I hope,
too that you will write another letter sometime to your
UNCLE E. A.

TO MRS. LOUIS V. LEDOUX

Peterborough, August 7, 1918
The last I heard of you was to the general effect that you
were somewhere on an island, and I am merciful enough to

hope that you are still there. But for certain atmospheric complications, I could hope that you might knit socks at the bottom of the Atlantic Ocean until this infernal weather is over. By which you will see that I am still friendly and thoughtful. As a matter of fact, and contrary to my reputation as a cave-dweller, I have always been on the side of the sun-worshippers; though I may have a tendency to execute my devotions under a broad rimmed hat—especially when the Orb—like the Bee in *Our Mutual Friend*—has a tendency to overdo it. He got so bad about a week ago that I wrote a poem of 24 lines with two suicides in it. On the whole I have continued after a fashion to create my own atmosphere as you call it, and to do rather more work than I had in view up to this time. If things go on as they are going, I might be able to throw together a small book by the end of the year, but I foresee that I shall have sense enough not to do it. I am inclined to believe more and more in my old dictum regarding one book of poetry in five years; but as that method implies the existence of conditions more favorable to leisure and longevity than mine have been since I began to lead a better life, I shall hardly attempt to do for myself, in the way of publication, what I recommend for others. With L. & G. and this new book out of the way I may inaugurate that peanut stand which I have had in mind ever since I gave up going to New Zealand. But I forgot that you don't know all about my more material ambitions. There is a woman here from New Zealand who tells me that the pseudo-socialism now prevalent there is a dead failure. I had even fancied that I might fit there as a dish-washer or a ticket chopper—if they have 'em—but that dream is about over now. The peanut stand is the only vision left that stays put.

What Frenchman was it who said that modern philosophy taught us to admire the unintelligible where we had better be satisfied with the unknown? I don't know that this has any direct bearing on poetry, as such, or on peanuts, or on anything in particular. Give my best regards to your good man and tell him to write me a letter. And do you likewise whenever the war gets you too hard. I am the joyfullest person to write to that ever lived.

TO MRS. LAURA E. RICHARDS

Peterborough, August 29, 1918

I know it—so please forgive me once more. Besides which, when I don't, you don't have to read my writing. I have always admired John for his integrity, as well as for his more engaging qualities, but I have never considered him intrinsically as a writer of elegiacs, which I found in the *Outlook* and read with real—not simulated or perfunctory —satisfaction. I didn't know that he did such things, not having seen 'em before. . . .

I hope your sick animals are all well again and that you are all enjoying the blessings, such as they are, of a busted world. I still feel like a civil worm when I let myself think about it, but as a result of not too much thinking I have continued to get together, somehow or other, the better part of another book. Whether such unpopular wares as mine should be put on the market these days is a thing for me to consider—not that it makes the slightest kind of difference whether they are exposed or not. In about 50 years from now there will be a small paragraph somewhere to this effect: "E. A. R., born, etc. He expected to die young, and should have done so. Owing, however, to some slight cosmic error, he was allowed to live beyond the logical time and to write divers books of verse, mostly about corpses and things, and lost illusions—never having had any of his own worth mentioning. For about ten years of his life he drank too much rum (chiefly as a more or less ingenious occupation for his idle hours, which began at noon and ended any time between two and five in the morning). He wrote some fairly good metres, at times, and he died owing money. When he was gone, his friends—of whom, for some altogether un-explained reason, he had several, in spite of the fact that he never said anything to them to let them know how much he liked them—all said, in a sort of hesitating unison: 'Well,' with a rising inflexion. He was unpopular during his life, on account of his incurable optimism, which was al-ways a source of wonder to those who did not know better. Many seemed to think that he should have fussed and cussed more than he did for having been born to such an ornery lot as that of an 'intellectual poet'—when, as a matter of fact, anything like a proper comprehension of his product was, and is—so far as it is at all—a matter of feel-ing, not of cerebration. It has taken a long time to find this out, and a few of the prodigiously faithful are still at it."

O good Lord, I'm not going to read that over. If I do, I know I shan't send it—in which case, all my good inten-tions in the way of writing some sort of fool letter will have gone to the flames. I have a bully fire this afternoon, with a comfortable autumn drizzle outside. The *Atlantic* has a thing of mine called "The Valley of the Shadow," which is not in all ways what its name suggests. In some ways it's as cheerful as a Cheshire Cat.

With very great regard, I am

Torquato Tasso

TO HERMANN HAGEDORN

Peterborough, September 8, 1918

Hooray for Master Oakley Hagedorn. Also congratulations on the name. May he live long, etc., and not have to write. May he be an educator, or a surgeon, or a President of the United States, or an archer, or a franklin, or a silentiary, or anything other than a poet—that is, unless he has a lot of money. I find, on looking the word up to find out what it means, that he can't be a franklin exactly, but he may perhaps be something like one. Anyhow, I wish you all joy of his arrival, including his unsuspecting self.

I am much more than pleased with your suggestion about a possible article on the Arthurian poems, for I know that they will never be read until people are made to read them. Please don't tell Brett or Marsh that I said so. For they will agree with both hands in the air; and I hope to get them to bring out L. & G. next fall. In the meantime I can't make myself hope that the article had better be written until the poem is published—and I know that you won't misunderstand me. You are about right in regard to *Merlin*, except in his first motive. I have made him, without any legendary authority, such a lover of the world as to use Arthur and his empire as an object lesson to prove to coming generations that nothing can stand on a rotten foundation. If one insists, *Lancelot*, in this poem, and in L. & G., may be taken as a rather distant symbol of Germany, though the reader will do well not to make too much of this or to carry it too far. You missed the primary motive in Merlin's part and in all probability it was my fault that you did so, in spite of my making him state it twice in order to drive it home. Having it so clearly in my own mind, probably I permitted him to say it in too casual a manner—which would illustrate one of my forty-five worst failings. But the poem was written in anticipation of *L. & G.*, to complement its various incompletenesses, and the two should be read together. Whether they will be read at all or not, God, He knows. Galahad's "light" is simply the light of the Grail, interpreted universally as a spiritual realization of Things and their significance. I don't see how this can be made any more concrete, for it is not the same thing to any two individuals. The "torch of women" is to be taken literally. You seem to have both of them as I intended in your second reference to them in your letter. The most significant line in the two poems, considered from a purely practical point of view, is, perhaps, "The world has paid enough for Camelot"—in *L. & G.* I'll be glad if you will read my new version of it when I get back to town. I have taken out most of the experimental dactyls and pterodactyls, and cut most of the long speeches. On the whole I think it is about 300 per centum better.

[Postscript]
Please tell Mrs. Dorothy that when I don't send her my regards it is because she has them already.

TO HERMANN HAGEDORN

810 Washington Avenue
October 17, 1918

Your telegram just received by mail. I should like to have time for a good talk about various matters—including *Lancelot* (which I will leave with you for a while) and your new idea. Merlin was undoubtedly suggested, in its form, by your Maze. I shall be in Westport Friday evening and will telephone from there.

I was a little hasty about our ground-listening President,

but I don't yet feel sure that he won't spill the beans. Long
life to you.

TO LEWIS M. ISAACS

810 Washington Avenue, Brooklyn
December 19, 1918

I have just received a note from Ledoux which puts me
again under great obligation to you and, as I understand
(or rather, don't understand), to others. Therefore, I must
ask you once more to say for me what I cannot say for
myself. I thought of this matter, naturally, when you wrote,
but I felt that I should be assuming too much knowledge
of your affairs if I intruded, without more data, my assurance of a friendship that does not change with the expira-
tion of exceptional favors. Of course it makes all the difference with my work that things are as they are, but if they
were otherwise (and I had more than a notion that they
might be) I should still be

Yours invariably (you can't read that, so I'll say it again):
Yours invariably

[Postscript]
This is entirely inadequate, but you may supply all that I
don't say.

TO MRS. MABEL DODGE STERNE

810 Washington Avenue
March 12, 1919

I was very glad to hear from you again and to learn that
you and the Indians are getting on so well together. What
you have to say of them is most interesting, for I have had

the same feeling all my life about the Orientals. If I knew the Indians, very likely I should feel about them as you do. Anyhow, I am sure that we white folks are doing the work while some farther-sighted race is waiting to show us what to do with what we have done—or maybe to exterminate us and do it themselves without our assistance or interference. Meanwhile we shall have the League of Nations to play with while Germany is getting herself and Russia together for another grand smash. You will see from this that I have no faith in any social scheme that doesn't see beyond a moonshine millennium. Sometimes I wonder if it would take much to set me yelling for an absolute monarchy in this country—assuming that we haven't got one. The world is a hell of a place; and if life and the universe mean anything, there is no reason to suppose that it will ever be anything else. This, as I understand it, is the true optimism. What would be the sense in living in a material world longer than one found it interesting?

TO MRS. JAMES EARLE FRASER

Peterborough, August 4, 1919

How are you all, and how are all the dogs? I am glad to report that my poetical horse is working again—overtime, in fact—and that I shall, in all probability, have something that may really be called a book when the product of this season is added to the rest. Last winter was a barren time with me, and I think it quite likely that I should have shot myself in disgust for not doing anything better if it hadn't been for the Frasers (whose hospitality I so cruelly overworked) and the sittings for that classic head (which came so near annihilation) and those theatres (which were very many times worse than any of us realized). Fortunately I can enjoy almost anything that a curtain goes up and down on. . . . I hope your mother is much better by this time, and that you are all on good terms with that intermittent and unreliable old rat-catcher, the Joy of Living. Just at present he is around the corner of my studio, with ferrets in his basket, waiting for me to find a word that means something between excellence and supremacy, and isn't greatness, and won't spoil a line. If I find it, he may come in and sit down.—I have a scene between Hamilton and Burr, which may possibly be interesting, though not so interesting as Fraser's Hamilton by himself—my description of which would seem to be a sort of double-headed ambiguity. You may take it either way you like—or both ways. I suppose your carrots are flourishing.

TO LEWIS M. ISAACS

Cornwall-on-Hudson
October 23, 1919

You may be interested to know that Roth's cheque for Five Hundred Dollars [1] came a few hours after my letter of yesterday went away. The book is to be published sometime this year, so he says, but he will have to change his methods in order to bring such an event to pass. I don't know who got the other two prizes, but have heard a rumor to the effect that one of them was likely to go to Sandburg, the singer of "blood and guts" and of much else appertaining to Chicago. The above quotation is taken from his text, though it isn't exactly original. He is a sweet singer, and one of the best, I am told, in Amy's jazz band.

TO PERCY MACKAYE

810 Washington Avenue
December 24, 1919

I shall have a lot to say to you when you come back to town again, but just now, on paper, I can only tell you that there are not many like you. Hagedorn and Ledoux hold you entirely responsible for some recent doings in the *Times;* [1] and if their accusations are correct, you have much to account for. So much, in fact, that I cannot even tell you how much. I wish it were possible for me to do so, but the Lord hasn't given the vocabulary or the brains.

My friends have always been a source of grateful wonder to me, but hereafter I shall lie awake o' nights trying to figure out what I have ever been or done, or been and gone and done, to deserve them. I see myself as the dullest duffer that ever lived, and often think of owing (as Torrence once put it) for a lodge in some vast wilderness. God knows I could never get it in any other way.

Apart from the trouble and labor that must have been involved in this remarkable enterprise of yours, let me thank you again, and apart, for your ripping article [2] in the *North American.* It is good to know that there are men alive like you, and sad to know that there are not many.

I'll try to say something better than this when I see you. In the meantime you have the best wishes that I can invent for you, and for you all—for this season and for all seasons.

Yours everlastingly,

TO MISS BARBARA ROBINSON [1]

810 Washington Avenue
January 18, 1920

I am doing my best to keep warm and will continue the process by acknowledging your letter. Please know that I am always glad to hear from any of you, although my way of showing it may not be altogether adequate. I had a letter not long ago from your mother who seems to be happier in her new place than she was in Boston. The Labrador attraction [2] is as much a mystery to me as it is to you, and I advise you not to give in to it.—Sometime or other I hope to see you all again—though a fellow in my business hasn't in the nature of things much to say for himself. When you are an old woman you may possibly begin to hear something about what I have been doing.

And I haven't forgotten to thank you for your Christmas present. When you write to Ruth [3] or Marie, [4] give them my love and tell them to write to me if they aren't mad at me for not writing to them. I think enough of you all to make up for my silence—only of course you don't know it.

TO MRS. LOUIS V. LEDOUX

Peterborough, June 24, 1920

It seems to me that your neighbor was eminently justified in making life unpleasant for a hired man who could laugh when his employer found that his gin was water and his whiskey tea; and I am a bit surprised that you and Louis should have the temerity to hire a fellow capable of such inhuman mirth at so tragic a moment. A creature of that sort is capable not only of treasons, strategems and spoils, but of almost anything else. You had better look out for your silver.

You may tell Louis that he has in me a fellow victim of poetic non-estness. I have drawn empty buckets from the Pierian reservoirs until my arms ache and my head swims, and at last have sought relief in a pretty good detective story. Fortunately the last of my *Taverns* proof goes back today, and that may make a difference—though I'm still afraid of a proof-reader who insists for the third time on changing "scared" to "sacred." Whenever this demon finds any poetry, he puts a query on the margin. But he doesn't find much. . . . Chekhof's letters are amazingly good, but I won't tell you so again.

You might ask Louis to write me a letter telling me everything that he knows about how to write poetry. I have buried its tail with salt, but it doesn't even wag—which introduces another figure. No matter—it's all the fault of that proof-reader. *Lancelot* seems to be rather well entreated, though not, for the most part, with any remarkable exhibition of intelligence.

Please write another letter when you cannot think of anything more exciting to do.

TO MRS. JAMES EARLE FRASER

Peterborough, August 6, 1920
. . . The failure of the photographs to appear has disquieted me somewhat, and has led me to fear that you might, at the eleventh or twelfth hour, have come to the wholly erroneous conclusion that the head isn't satisfactory to me. If I have given you, through my lack of vociferous enthusiasm, any cause to suspect that my enthusiasm is any

the less real (and I know well enough that I haven't) you have only to call me a clam or an oyster, and to remember the good qualities of both. To be brief and sensible, I am tickled to pieces with the head, and am properly pleased and surprised at the thought of your making a bronze of it. Only I didn't wish you and Jimmy to go to the expense of doing it, unless you are pretty sure that it will, in some mysterious way or other, be worth your while. I have been hoping to do it myself sometime, but just now, as I need hardly tell you, such a vainglorious luxury is altogether beyond me.

Looking at the thing impersonally, whether in bronze or in plaster, I don't see how it can fail to be a good thing for you to have on hand. And I know that Jimmy thinks so, for I have heard him say things about it that you weren't obliged to hear. And I wish to assure you again that the whole process was a most agreeable one for me; and that even if it had been less successful I should not be sorry—which is an infernally poor way of putting it. I am confident, however, that my willingness to hang around the Frasers' workshop, and to say now and then some wholly gratuitous things about sculpture, requires no sort of iteration or emphasis. I only wonder sometimes that I haven't been put out. . . .

I'm glad that you can read *Lancelot,* and feel somehow that the external tragedy of the cocktails is sadly appropriate. I had two the other evening when I went out to dinner—the first and only. The whole situation is awful, although there is a ray of hope. It appears that a barrel of cider, treated with a pound of sugar to the gallon, together with raisins, beefsteak and various other fauna and flora, may be converted into a regular reservoir of possibilities. You had better ask Sawyer to investigate and then let me pay for half the sugar. Descending to matters less important, you may be interested to know that my "Rembrandt" thing (about

350 lines) is now behind me, and that the poetical horse is still going—which means apparently that I have another book under way. The *Taverns* should be out in about a month. . . .

TO PERCY MACKAYE

Peterborough, September 29, 1920

I'm sorry not to see you before you go into your western retreat—where I trust you may find at least a part of what you deserve in the way of peace and opportunity.

Personally, I'm inclined to hope that you will see fit to chuck the new pageant—though I'm well aware of my hopeless limitations when anything with "Community" pasted on it rolls into sight. I'm a democrat in that I'm as likely to form a lifelong friendship with a coal-heaver as with a millionaire (rather more so, in fact), but there my democracy ends.

And as for the democratization of art, there ain't no such animal. Art may die, having served its purpose, but it will never be popular. The bare bones of great music will always hold the crowd, but they won't know what it is that holds them. We poor devils of poets must face the probability that there will never be more than one person in a thousand who will know or really care anything about poetry. The few people who make the world fit to live in are comparatively negligible, and they would be nothing without the others. I don't see what is to be done about it.

I'm sending along my *Taverns*, which you may like to consider after you are settled.

TO KERMIT ROOSEVELT

810 Washington Avenue
November 17, 1920

. . . As soon as my mortal frame becomes a little more flexible again, I shall be very glad to come to your home some evening, as you suggest. As a rule I refuse invitations to dinner—simply for altruistic reasons—though occasionally, as you know, I am glad to break my rule. Filling a place at a table is as much an art as the writing of sonnets, and, fortunately for this world, there are more who can do it well. Wherefore I feel that my conversational shortcomings require of me a pretty good sonnet—which I trust is once in a while forthcoming, though not just now.

TO LOUIS V. LEDOUX

810 Washington Avenue
December 14, 1920

I have been intending and intending, etc., until I have become one of the best intenders in Brooklyn, where there must be many. I won't make any more excuses, but still it is a fact that I am not yet more than in sight of the top of the hill that I rolled down when the grippe got me. Two friends of mine have been cheering me up by telling me that it was three months before they could lift their feet without thinking it over. So much for my infirmities.— Lately I've been tinkering some sonnets and getting my dime novel ready for possible spring publication. It looks now as if it would be followed in the fall by the collected works of E. A. R.—God help him—the paper of which will in all probability be manufactured from the gray fibre of

E. A. R.'s unhappy soul. There's a silver lining to all this, too. When I saw what a rotten looking book the *Tavern* was doomed to be, I felt pretty sure that it would have to sell, if only out of poetic justice, and now Brett tells me that a second edition is on the way. Well, it will be something to have it all together, and if it lives, no doubt it will eventually find a tailor. And all this talk of one's work "living" begins to amuse me as I grow old enough to think. Give Shakespeare 50,000 years—which he won't get—and then look at a megatherium or two, and where are we? Fortunately I don't believe in time, and so I'm all right. Meanwhile I shall have brightened the way for a few groping wanderers without lanterns, and shall have comforted them with the assurance that, generally speaking, they haven't a damned thing to say about it. Somehow or other I suspect that my rather rickety existence has justified itself, but I don't recommend its equivalent to anyone else. I wish to die without an evil thought for any of my kind, and so I hope that the Lord in His eternal wisdom will never make another one like Me. Mr. Flood, who was turned down for alcoholic reasons by *Collier's*, made his disreputable debut in the *Nation* (no reflection on the *Nation*, though I don't agree with its politics) and is going along with all this other valuable language in the hope of finding you and Jean at home in a pagoda, eating beetle-grubs and birds' nests, and having a wonderful time. . . .

TO MRS. LOUIS V. LEDOUX

810 Washington Avenue
February 3, 1921

I gather from your two letters that you are continuing, in spite of your mishaps, to have a good time. Don't have any more of them if you can help it, and don't let Louis become so thoroughly Orientalized as to insist on making a Chinese lady of you. I can't get wholly over a suspicion that he has intended all along to buy a pagoda and eventually have a pigtail—in which event you would have a new addition to your family cares, for he could never take care of the thing. You would have to braid it and twist it for him. But on second thought, I seem to have heard that pigtails aren't worn any more by the best people. Speaking of China, I heard *Tristan* the other evening, for the first time in about six years. They sang it in English, but about all the English I caught was "What thinkst thou of yon minion" and "Behold our flag is flying"—which helped some. Incidentally, someone has been whispering to Bodansky, for he put more ginger into the orchestra than he did at first. There's a new ship, about the size of the *Mauretania,* and a new tree—in fact a new arrangement altogether for the last act, by which the fight (the worst at best on any stage) is practically done away with. Only one stone is used for a homicide and that isn't a very big one. Kurvenal does not even look on, but stands with his back to the whole row, such as it is, apparently admiring the new Metropolitan ocean, and finally turns around in order to get his mortal wound. Isolde (Florence Easton) has another innovation. Instead of falling down on Tristan, where she belongs, she lays herself carefully about three feet away from him with her head at his feet. I don't approve of that and don't believe that Wagner would. On the whole the thing went very well and there wasn't room in the house for an extra sardine. For a few hours I fancied that our so-called civilization might not be going after all—though of course it is. The whole western world is going to be blown to pieces, asphyxiated, and starved, and then, for a few centuries we poor artists are going to have a hard time. There may not be any, in fact, for they will have either to die or to dig; and if they dig they can't compose any Tristans, or paint any pictures, or write any poetry. If they did, no one would pay any attention, for all the rest would be too much occupied with staying alive. Sometimes I indulge my ego to the extent of wondering whether any of my mortal works will survive the smash. Not that it would signify much if they did.—Last evening at a dinner in town I met Colonel Whittlesey—the "go to hell" man of the Lost Battallion (only one "I"? I can't spell any more, and so must be growing old) and liked him. Apart from cussing the Germans in good set terms, it appears that he reads poetry, or says he does—even mine. But I'm always rather skeptical of strangers, especially heroes, when they say that. This reminds me that I have just got myself into trouble by agreeing to write a Pilgrims' Chorus for the coming Plymouth Pageant. If I do it at all, the only good feature of it will be the hundred dollars that I'm supposed to get for it. Cale Young Rice could do it better. My dime novel[1] has gone to the printer, and the *Collected Poems of E. A. R.* is under way. Evidently I'm getting ready to depart, but I don't want to go this winter. There will be things to do to the proofs. May you and Louis live long, but not too long in China.

Pax vobiscum.

TO AMY LOWELL

810 Washington Avenue
May 12, 1921

At the risk of making too much of nothing, I wish to assure you that the enclosed,[1] which has just been sent to me, happens to be entirely mistaken. I did make such a remark, in a joking way, about free verse in general, and was quoted to that effect in the *Times,* but I did not have your poetry in mind, and did not make even the remotest reference to you or to your work. These things are annoying, even though they be of no importance.

TO ARTHUR DAVISON FICKE

Peterborough, June 11, 1921

I did not hear of ———'s death until a day or two ago, when I surmised at once that he had assisted nature in removing him from a world that somehow never had a place for him. Your verses were an astonishing representment of the man, and I am very glad to have them. I intended to see ——— before I left New York, but one thing and another turned up to prevent my doing so. All of which I regret intensely, for I believe that he really cared a great deal for me in his obscure way. He must have suffered hell during his latter days, but I know almost nothing of the circumstances. His marriage was, I fancy, rather a disaster, like almost everything else that came his way; and yet he had a singular vein of practical energy that enabled him to extract a living from this world, and in regions where I, for one, would have starved. All told, he was the strangest being I ever knew, and at the same time one of the most fascinating and (I may as well be honest) in some ways one of the most unhuman. He may have been inhuman, also, but he was never that to me. So peace to him, wherever and whatever he is now. There was much in him that was good, and the rest is not, as you say, our affair. I hope to see you this winter—also Bynner, who is now, I infer, about half a Chinaman.

TO ARTHUR DAVISON FICKE

Peterborough, June 23, 1921

Apropos of your second note, and of ———'s end, I have lately received a letter from one of his son's intimate friends in which there is no reference to ———'s making away with himself, or any suggestion of it. . . . So far as I am concerned it makes no particular difference how he went— by which I mean that it makes no difference in my feeling for the man. A suicide signifies discouragement or despair— either of which is, or should be, too far beyond the scope of our poor piddling human censure to require of our ig- norance anything less kind than silence. I still have a sus- picion that he helped things along, but whether he did or not is no matter. In all this I am sure that you will agree with me. . . .

TO WITTER BYNNER

810 Washington Avenue
October 14, 1921

I am grateful to know that you approve of Mr. Flood.[1] For I have a somewhat prejudiced liking for him myself; and I thank you for taking the trouble to write to me about him. And this reminds me of your two books, which were received and read, but—to my shame and sorrow—never properly acknowledged. I said this in a letter to Ficke who may or may not have passed the word on to you, and am just as grateful to you as if I had written sooner about them. As I told Ficke, I got far more pleasure from the last book than from the one before it, but very likely that was due to my attitude, apparently constitutional, towards free verse.

I am pretty well satisfied that free verse, prohibition, and moving pictures are a triumvirate from hell, armed with the devil's instructions to abolish civilization—which, by the way, has not yet existed, and cannot exist until the human brain undergoes many changes. A brain, for example, that is 100% American cannot in the nature of things have many percent left over.

TO RIDGELY TORRENCE

810 Washington Avenue
December 16, 1921

Your lyrical reception of my barge [1] makes me hope that the thing may stay afloat, at least for a while. And even if it should become waterlogged, I still hope that a few planks and hen-coops may continue to get themselves washed ashore. But the Lord only knows about that. We're out in a rough sea. In the meantime I am very much obliged to you for your welcome. . . .

TO JOHN DRINKWATER

810 Washington Avenue
February 3, 1922

. . . I am naturally greatly pleased that you should have given a lecture on my poetry to an audience that had never heard of me, and my gratitude for your loyalty is mixed with admiration for your courage. If the lecture is printed, as you say it may be, you may be sure that I shall read it with an uncommon interest. I don't know how to thank you, but you will understand all that.

Please give my kindest regards to the Ervines [1] and tell

Mrs. Drinkwater that I have never seen the snapshot that you took on Fifth Avenue. Incidentally you might give her my regards also. I saw the Ledoux (*les* Ledoux would be easier) last evening, and we spoke of both your houses—though in a wholly non-Mercutian sense. When are we to see you again? And did you receive my Big Book? Ervine tells me in a pleasant note that he received his, but you avoid the subject. If you didn't get it, please let me know, and I'll see that you don't escape.

[Postscript]
Thank you also for John o' London's remarks, for which you are plainly responsible.

TO MRS. LAURA E. RICHARDS

Peterborough, August 15, 1922
I'm sorry to say that I don't know *Bugbee's Collection,* and that there are still a few other things that I don't know. I didn't know until today, for example, that curfew means cover the fire. Perhaps you did know it, but I doubt if you know what a luce is. It has nothing to do with the lucifugous Thomas Hardy—whose last book of poems, by the way, is most remarkable. Apparently he will take his place among the solid poets of England, which is a pretty good place to take. He and Francis Thompson are, so far as I can see, the only real figgers (both of the second order, I suppose) since Swinburne, who isn't any too real—except in a few places. Whatever led you to suppose that I read Greek? I had a few scraps of it, but, *ai, ai,* no more.

TO MRS. LAURA E. RICHARDS

Peterborough, August 24, 1922

I don't know how I came to leave out Kipling, but apparently because he was so big that I didn't see him. You would be pleased, or so I infer, if you knew how much I pity the whippersnappers who are now beginning to patronize him. Dickens, who could have put them all in his porridge and eaten them without knowing anything about it, they would dismiss entirely. Poor children. But Galileo was right, and it still moves. There was a brief time, years ago, when I—may the Lord have long forgiven me—chivied myself into a sort of notion that Dickens and Wagner were "going"—and so they are, going strong. Hardy's poetry, by the way, fares about as badly with a single reading as that of another spreader of sunshine whom I might drag in.

Your most respectful

E. A. R.

TO MRS. LAURA E. RICHARDS

28 West 8th Street
March 2, 1923

I don't believe there is any need of worrying over cheerful Mr. Housman. When I had read three pages of his first book, years ago, I knew that he had come to stay. The second book isn't quite so good, but that doesn't matter. His kingdom is a small and not very jolly one, but he is the boss of it, and that's enough. . . .

TO MISS ROSALIND RICHARDS

Garland's Hotel, Suffolk St., Pall Mall
May 18, 1923

It was good to get your letter on arriving here and to know that you are all well. I am well enough, but London too obviously isn't. The place is so hard up that one feels it in the air and gets a disquieting sense of things that are past. Maybe I should have had the same impression ten years ago, but somehow I don't think so. Don't imagine from this that I am not enjoying myself, for that would be a great mistake. When I go to Oxford, probably in a few weeks, I rather expect to settle down for the summer and do some work. The process of travel is such a bore to me that I don't even go so far as to think of seeing Paris or Rome. People are more than places to me—though I am glad that you like the river in *R. B.*[1] You should know it pretty well by this time, for you have lived near it all your life, and the house.[2] I'm not sure that the Gardiners would approve of the people that I have put into it.

TO LOUIS V. LEDOUX

3, Hertford Street, Mayfair, W.1.
June 11, 1923

I could easily stay in England for the rest of my life, but unfortunately can foresee that I should never do any work. Old and New England would be forever fighting for the upper hold—and there is something in me that for practical purposes doesn't transplant. The more I see of the country the more I like it—and London still more. Doctor Johnson was right. The length of time that I am over here will not be so important as the fact that I shall have been here for a while. Without any change of air there would never have been any peace for my troubled soul. Therefore you needn't be surprised if you hear of my returning sometime in August. The good Frasers seem really (God knows just why) to want me again in the fall; and while London makes New York look like a box of soap, there is still much in New York that one doesn't readily forget.

Drinkwater is so prosperous it makes me blink to look at him. His *Cromwell* is a big success and his *Lee,* which opens about the 20th, may easily be another. He is the happiest man in the world, so far as I know, and it is pretty obvious that his happiness is not founded altogether on gold or glory. . . . I had luncheon the other day with the Ervines, by the way, and found the Lamonts, whom you know. Also I met Miss Grigsby at the opening of *Cromwell,* and was gratified to be told by her that she "treasured" my two lines in her birthday book. Well, I hope she does—for they are, in their way, among the best that I have written.

[Postscript]
Garland's was all right for a while, but finally got on my nerves. This place is no more expensive and far more like a place to live in. And the chairs are more like things to sit in. That makes me realize that the call of the rocker is still in me, and would be if I were to stay here for a hundred years.

TO LEWIS M. ISAACS

3 Hertford Street, Mayfair, W.1.
July 9, 1923
. . . Everything has gone wonderfully with me, but about two weeks ago I began to be aware that it was time for me to get

down to work again, and that I had really got what I came for. Therefore I find the call of Peterboro stronger than that of England and Europe together, and I've decided to sail away on the 21st if there's a place for me on the *President Adams*. I shall be very sorry to miss seeing you, but as my going at this time will give me two months in the woods, I find it impossible for me to square my conscience with another six weeks of expensive loafing and the additional cost of nothing done and very likely nothing started. My hope is to get my new book really going in August and September and keep at it through the winter; and I am sure that you will agree with me in saying that there is no particular sense in my staying over here if I'm going to be dissatisfied with myself for doing so. . . .

TO LEWIS M. ISAACS

Peterborough, August 9, 1923

Although I was sorry in many ways to leave England, I have to confess to myself that it is rather good to be back in this place again. I arrived early yesterday afternoon and so don't know much about the newcomers. . . . Whatever you do or don't do, you must go to Cambridge and see King's College Chapel. I'm not much in the way of a sight-seer—but that thing isn't a sight, it's just a miracle. If I had been born in England I know exactly what I should think of America—with no reflections on either country. . . .

[Postscript]

If you care to walk up Wood Street from Cheapside, you may like to stop at Silver and Monkwell Streets, where Shakespeare is supposed to have lived for some seven years. Anyhow, the Mermaid was in Cheapside below Bread and Friday, and all the old boys were there, before the fire.

TO MRS. LAURA E. RICHARDS

Peterborough, August 10, 1923

. . . I found England a strangely foreign sort of place that was strangely like home. If I had been born there I should have some very special opinions of this country, but having been born here, I have to acknowledge that New England is in my blood and bones, and will not be denied. All the same, London makes New York look like Uncle Sam's backyard; and England itself is probably nearer to paradise (on the surface) than any other part of this wale. One gets a notion over there that the whole thing is going, but it isn't doing anything of the sort. But it surely is changing.

TO LEWIS M. ISAACS

Peterborough, August 25, 1923

. . . It is good to know that your trip has been so generally a good experience for you all—though I suffered for you in Italy while I was stewing in London during the heat. In your letter you tried at least to make me believe that you enjoyed it, from which we could only gather that you had nothing like the damnable three weeks that descended upon perfidious Albion. Perfidious in its own way, perhaps, in the past, but it is the best thing that we have now, even though tired out and dead broke. I see in France a sort of short-sighted Samson, and wonder when the roof is going to fall—assuming that there is any roof left. Down here in the woods it is easy to be a prophet and to say that all this chatter about peace will continue to be imbecility so long as there are custom houses in the world. I am getting gradually down to work and somehow or other hope to have another book of short things. I'll see you all in October.

TO RIDGELY TORRENCE

Peterborough, August 30, 1923

I was glad to get your letter and to hear that you found a way to print G.'s poem, which I still say is a pretty good one—surely a damned sight better than *Black Eyed Susan*, which for some reason is immortal. . . .

I am trying to write sonnets, but when I consider that there are only about forty or fifty really good ones in the world, I wonder if I hadn't better be delivering milk. But that wouldn't do, for I shouldn't like the hours.

TO MRS. LAURA E. RICHARDS

Peterborough, June 2, 1924

If you will make *Ariel* [1] your thirty-eighth book for this date it will be quite satisfactory. As a preparation for a long stretch of work, I have been going through *Our Mutual Friend, Little Dorrit, Copperfield,* and *Great Expectations* —though I don't say that the last-named signifies anything. Barring the inevitable Victorian stickiness, they still go surprisingly well. But one has to skip Dora. I'm not sure that the Wrayburn-Headstone business is not the best melodrama in English—though I still stand up for *Bleak House*. The only one that I can't go back to is *Nickleby*—which of course has to contain some of the author's best work, along with most of his worst.

I have also been reading the Old Testament, a most bloodthirsty and perilous book for the young. Jehovah is beyond a doubt the worst character in fiction.

[Postscript]

I remember reading your "Titus" poem in one of your books.

TO MRS. LAURA E. RICHARDS

Peterborough, July 11, 1924

I am inclined to believe that Nietzsche will last for some time to come, though there may be no reason why you should wade through the whole of *Zarathustra* as I did. *Beyond Good and Evil* is more important, though riddled by the same worms. One half of N. is great, the other half gangrened. Maybe you will like better the following lines by one Lionel Glover [1]:

> *"The human soul a tortoise is*
> *Lured by the warm eve's dewy kiss:*
> *It ventures out its peering neck*
> *To greet the outer world and thwack!*
> *The injurious God from ambush out*
> *Visits the soft defenceless snout."*

Yours for today
E. A. R.

TO MRS. LAURA E. RICHARDS

Peterborough, July 20, 1924

You must have confused my alleged strictures of *Great Expectations* with what I may have said of some other book. It is one of the best stories that we have, and I couldn't possibly have said much against it. Miss Havisham is a bit of a strain, yet somehow or other Dickens manages to pull her through—all but the wedding cake, which the various recorded vermin would have consumed long before the story began. I'm not sure that *Our Mutual Friend* isn't about as good as any of the books—as I may have said before.

I have just finished the first draft of a poem (about the length of *The Man Against the Sky*) about Dionysus—which you won't like, although I hope you may like my way of doing it. It had to come out, for it has been accumulating within me ever since the hypocritical (or worse) action of the so called Supreme Court on the constitutionality of a certain much to be damned amendment—which, by the way, doesn't affect me personally. I beg your pardon, but this is just how it appears to me; and you wouldn't wish me to be so large a liar at my advanced age as to pretend otherwise. One hundred men, who have all they want stored away in their cellars, could probably put an end to the whole business if they dared to open their mouths except to take a drink.

As for the rest, it's a beautiful day, and I shall be glad to have the *Speculators,* as I am always

Your obedient servant
Appius Claudius

P. S. "One stone struck Appius on the mouth."

TO MRS. LAURA E. RICHARDS

Peterborough, July 31, 1924

Your quotations are apt enough, surely, and might also be adequate if it were possible for me to see things differently. As for my sympathies, I have always supposed them to be, if possible, a little too inclusive. In fact they include almost anything save what I understand to be an organized violation of first principles. The familiar argument that alcohol belongs in the same class with drugs (not that you mention any such nonsense) is too silly for serious discussion. All human beings who are not made of putty are going to stimulate themselves in one way or another; and alcohol, in spite of its dangers, is the least harmful of all the more active demons. Everything is dangerous that is worth having. For example, think of poetry and music, not to mention fried onions and cucumbers. Dr. Schumann [1] was a fairly successful and contented local doctor until poetry got him at about the age of thirty. The rest of his life was a slow débâcle, if there is such a thing, and he would have died poor, without the aid of rum (which he never "abused") if he hadn't married some money. And all on account of poetry. If you need any further example of a life wrecked on the foaming reefs of song, consider the worldly voyage of

Your most obedient
E. A. R.

[Postscript]

There is no danger of my forgetting the change in your house. If I don't mention it, you will understand that I don't know what to say.[2]

TO MRS. LAURA E. RICHARDS

Peterborough, August 16, 1924

Did I forget to mention the Catullus translation to which you called my attention in the *Spectator?* Probably I did; and if so, I'll say that the specimen offered did not impress me as particularly happy. If C. were alive and knew English he would retch at "Sirmio dear" and shake his head at the rest. Poetry cannot be translated anyhow, and maybe Catullus and Heine—who are in some ways related—least of all. About the only thing to do is to dust off whatever Latin we have left and read him with a literal translation. With my pin-feather knowledge of Italian I can read Dante in this way and apparently get most of him. But I can't say that of Latin, for I don't remember enough of it; and there is also the diabolical arrangement of the words. Greek, being far less crazy in its construction, is easier to follow.— As for my Lord Byron, I don't know what to say, considering life as the hopelessly mixed up and imperfect mess that it is. The episode to which you refer would seem to prove him a complete rotter, but on the other hand he was generous and even democratic with his friends, and apparently was as fond of Shelley as he could be of anybody but himself. If we knew all the circumstances (which we never do) perhaps there might be found at least a passive or scratchy defence for his action, or lack of it. I don't remember all the circumstances, as reported, and I don't remember anything in the nature of a motive. Even if the charge were true, and he knew it, he should have lied like a gentleman, even though he wasn't one. Whenever a celebrity is pelted in the market place, and his every offence and error is exposed and magnified in letters of fire, I think of certain quiet and eminently respectable citizens of my acquaintance whose achievements would make Byron's appear almost like those of a bad boy at school. Being what he was, he was egregiously "sought arter" and must many a time have felt that he was making a fool of himself in trying to be decent. And maybe, like Sam Weller's father, he didn't "take out no pride on it". He was a bounder, no doubt, but his heritage accounts for a good deal—though the incident in question is apparently pretty nasty. Wagner is another who could not possibly have found the time to be so wicked as his enemies would have him. Mrs. Perry is still unable to see anything good in his music because he wasn't a good man. The new life of Beethoven by Thayer gave her a most awful jolt, but it was rather too late for her to change her mind.

TO MRS. LAURA E. RICHARDS

Peterborough, September 21, 1924

A. Oh no, I don't want the world drunk. On the other hand, I don't want a world tyrannized by Henry Fords, W. J. Bryans, and Charles W. Eliots—which appears to be on the way. If it's destiny, it will come, but thank God I'll be dead.

B. It would be gey queer, but better than a permanent and impregnable Chautauqua, how do you spell it?

C. I still fear that you confuse wisdom and knowledge. One who is otherwise comparatively a fool may have more wisdom than the most learned scholar or technician . . . or doctor.

D. I may send you one of the *Dionysus* poems (there are two—one about prohibition and the other about spurious democracy) before long—when I have them typed.

E. I expect to leave here on October fourth. After a few days in Boston my address will be 28 West 8th St., New York.

F. There are worse places.

G. I have also the honour to remain,—though I am beginning to wonder just why,

Yours very sincerely

T.(orquato)T.(asso)

[Postscript]
I'm returning the marked *Spectator*. Please send the next batch to New York. Always many thanks.

TO MRS. LAURA E. RICHARDS

[no date]

I am enclosing the first of my two *Dionysus* poems, which will probably make you sniff, sneer, and snort. No matter— you will at least know what my sentiments are, and you may possibly like the verse, as such. Please return it to Peterborough sometime before October first, and so oblige

Yours abstemiously

(for the present, at any rate)

T. T.

TO MRS. JAMES EARLE FRASER

28 West 8th Street
November 18, 1924

. . . Maybe I have a sort of subconscious realization of having written enough of my sort, but even then the habit is probably too strong for me to break, and you will have to go on reading books of mine until you are an old lady with an ear-trumpet. I don't quite see you as an old lady, but you will be one some day, I suppose, with all sorts of people waiting on you and singing your many deserved praises. If I live to be ninety or so, I may come tottering in sometimes myself, still beaming and happy, as always, and still smoking Sweet Caporal cigarettes to the frowning despair and consternation of the young. They give me dark and dubious looks even now, and continue to smoke Camels.

We have had only one theater so far, and the show was so bad that we were almost glad, for the moment, that you were in Paris where you couldn't see it. Even now the house isn't really settled, and it won't be like itself until you come back

—though of course we are really glad on your account that you are where you are, and having such a fine time. Jimmy tells me that your latest plan, in possibility, is one of going to Egypt, where you will find the Sphinx and the pyramids very much the same and will have to ride on a camel. I have visions of your organizing a camel polo-team, with all Egypt for a field. You mustn't regard this infantile maundering in the light of a letter—my wits are still too fragmentary for that—but sometime before long I'll try to be a bit more coherent. . . . Jimmy is working on Jefferson in the next room, and the shades of night are falling fast. . . .

TO MRS. LAURA E. RICHARDS

28 West 8th Street
January 19, 1925

I have again the dishonor to report that I am an epistolary varlet. But I thank you all the same for your Christmas greetings, and for the *Spectators,* and for many more other things than it is possible for me to enumerate this side the next world. If there shouldn't happen to be any next world, or any that we remember (which I am inclined to believe and hope) we shall go on somehow or other. I get no comfort out of turning into grass, and cannot believe that the great Whatever-it-is would have gone to so much trouble as to make you and me (not to mention a few others) for the sake of a little ultimate hay.

Yours respectfully
T. T.

TO MRS. JAMES EARLE FRASER

99 St. Botolph Street, Boston
April 16, 1925

After reading your letter and considering the plan of "my" room, I'm afraid there is nothing for me to do but to give in. The thought of being with you all again another winter gives me much that is pleasant to anticipate, and it is pleasant to be told that my presence in the past has not been too much for you. Anyhow, I have tried not to make a great deal of noise. . . . And this reminds me that I can still make a little more trouble for you—to the extent of asking if you will be kind enough—any time before May 10th to send me the *Blue Guide to London* which you will find on the shelves up stairs. I'm not going to London, but sometimes I like to take up that book. It is almost as exciting as an illustrated seed-catalogue, and far more reliable. . . .

TO RIDGELY TORRENCE

99 St. Botolph Street
May 11, 1925

I have been waiting for your book before acknowledging your letter for which I thank you most respectful. I'm glad that you like the new book—or parts of it—and all that you say about the prize money [1] is appreciated. Whether you want it or not, I don't see how it can fail to come to you automatically next year. I have had a new pair of steel arches made for my feet and hope to be happy with them sometime. The doctor doesn't think much of my feet, and so I'm glad if I shine a little at the other end. . . .

TO LEWIS M. ISAACS

Peterborough, June 26, 1925

My "doctoring" was simply a matter of going to Bowdoin College for another degree. I supposed the Frasers understood about that, but apparently my incurable obscurity found a way into my letter to them. After that academic process, I went to Gardiner for a few days, and found a few surviving friends and relatives and a town considerably changed. Also I went down to Head Tide and saw for the first time in my memory the house where I had the questionable privilege of being born. It was a satisfaction to find the house still in good condition after having prepared myself to confront a typical New England ruin. The inhabitants were away, and so I couldn't get inside. The trip on the whole made me a little melancholy, but I'm glad for having made it and I'm glad to be back here again. For the present my work is knocked galley west. But no doubt my brain cells will readjust themselves in the course of a few days and give *Tristram* another chance. I'm glad that you are seeing the Frasers and hope that Westport may prove to be congenial. And I still hope that you and Mrs. Isaacs will find your way down here before the season is over. Some weeks ago I saw Marian [1] cutting respectable capers on the stage in Cambridge.

TO MRS. LAURA E. RICHARDS

Peterborough, July 26, 1925

Please don't annoy and depress me by talking about "going". In these days people of your age are just beginning to think and to look about them. The only reason why I am quiet and senile is because I don't like pizon, or the movies, or jazz bands. As a consequence I shall go long before either of you do. For that matter, this thing that I am doing now should be enough to carry me off. The fool potion, or philtre in the Tristram story has always been an incurable source of annoyance to me, and after fighting it away for four or five years I have finally succumbed to telling the story of what might have happened to human beings in those circumstances, without their wits and wills having been taken away by some impossible and wholly superfluous concoction. Men and women can make trouble enough for themselves without being denatured and turned into robots. The story will remain pretty much unchanged in its main outlines—but still with a difference. I shall get myself disliked for doing it, but I am rather used to that after *Merlin* and *Lancelot,* and so am not worrying on that score.—I don't see why you should be surprised at the outbreak of any sort of imbecility in this country, where imbeciles are so obviously in command.

TO LEWIS M. ISAACS

Peterborough, July 29, 1925

I haven't heard from you for some time and you haven't heard from me. The chief reason for the latter is that I have been pegging away so hard at *Tristram* that my correspondence has been reduced, for the most part, to a few compulsory notes. My only object in writing this poem is to get out of my system a long imprisoned curiosity to find out what sort of story might be made of T. and I. on the assumption that they were not necessarily a pair of impossible and irresponsible morons. Even with Wagner's music, the love potion makes the whole story silly for me. Men and

women can make trouble enough for themselves in this world
without being drugged into permanent imbecility. That
damned dose has always spoiled one of the world's greatest
stories and probably will continue to do so. I don't expect to
produce any change of opinion here any more than I did in
writing about prohibition—though I hope here as I did there,
to write a poem that can be read. But God only knows—
perhaps I have written more than enough already. And perhaps this means that I have been driving the horse a little too
hard and had better read Martin's *House of Souls*, which has
just come to me. I hope that you and Madam will find your
way down here before the summer is over. Let me hear from
you now and then.

TO MRS. LOUIS V. LEDOUX

Peterborough, August 3, 1925

. . . I haven't anything in particular to say for myself
except that *Tristram* still grows in length, like a serpent,
and doesn't seem to me to be in every way bad. The key and
color of the thing are altogether different from those of
Merlin and *Lancelot* and may cause some readers to suspect
that I'm getting a little tired of hearing too much about my
New England reticence—which may be pretty true. Just
now T. is under a tree in the rain, trying to get his wits
sufficiently together to remember the name of Isolt. When
he comes to himself, he is going to be getting out of a fever
in a shepherd's hut, and then that peculiar lady Queen
Morgan is going to carry him off to her house and keep him
for a while. When he gets away from her he is going over to
Brittany and marry the other Isolt, but he isn't going to
stay there always. It ought to be a pretty good poem (which
reminds me, not ominously, I hope) of the famous likeness,

attributed to Copeland of Harvard, of a pretty good poem to a pretty good egg. Anyhow, I'll do it as well as I can and look to all the gods for help. . . .

TO MISS ESTHER WILLARD BATES

Peterborough, August 3, 1926

. . . I'm glad you like Morgan's letter,[1] for I have sunk so far as to wish that I might write as good a one myself. Lancelot was good enough to give Tristram his country home for the summer, and went there with him from Camelot, all of which may be made a little clearer. . . . For some reason or other I am having more trouble with the catastrophe part than with anything else—chiefly, I fancy, on account of a possibly too acute fear of letting it run over into sentimentality—which is far worse than death. I have already killed them three times, but they are like cats with nine lives, and I may have to kill them nine times. . . .

TO MRS. LOUIS V. LEDOUX

Peterborough, September 2, 1926

. . . What I really want is a large city with everything available in it in the way of the arts and with about six people in it for me to see from time to time. If you know of such a metropolis please tell me about it.—As for visiting, something definite and specific has been happening inside me during the past three or four years, and the result is that I can't visit any more for longer than a few days. I have had to cut the Perrys short and shall have to excuse myself somehow from the Frasers and the Isaacs and two or three others. I shall be fifty-eight years old in December, and may as well face the truth that my habits, mostly bad, are not so flexible and adaptable as they were once. In most ways I don't feel any older than I did twenty years ago, but there are a few ways in which I am getting to be hopelessly "sot"—and one of them is an entirely selfish way of avoiding, so far as possible, the restraints and constraints that seem to be an unavoidable part of change. I don't want to travel— unless I can see a case of Scotch at the end of my journey (and as I'm on the wagon now, even that wouldn't do any good) and I don't want to visit even my friends for more than a few days. I hope that both of you will understand this. If you don't, you will before long. And before long I shall in all probability break loose for a month or so and go to Montreal or Bermuda or somewhere to a place that has a non-poisonous bar, and hasn't the shadow of imbecility hanging over it like doom. I have finished *Tristram* and am now ready to go to sleep like a woodchuck for about a month before I emerge and see people again. Boston is an admirable place for that.—There wasn't much left of T. and I. in my story when Andred stabbed T. in the back. The newspapers are still full of similar yarns, but they are no longer the fashion in literature. This thing of mine may be clubbed out of existence, or it may be welcomed as a sort of mint julep after too many years of dirty water which is the fashion. Anyhow, it will have to go as it may. . . .

IV

THE GARLAND

(Aetat. 57–65)

New York, March 14, 1927

Thank you for your letter and for your sonnet—which goes well and says something. Only please don't make two syllables of "fire".

I haven't heard of any recent disturbance among the Elysian Dwellers, and I doubt if there has been any; and I don't quite make out from your writing whether this sonnet is over a battle- or a bottle burnished name. But these are trifling matters, and I like to infer from your pleasant ironies that some things that I have written have given you some sort of pleasure. *Captain Craig* had an external original, more or less, but the other people are entirely imaginary, so far as I can say.

TO MRS. LAURA E. RICHARDS

328 East 42nd Street,
April 30, 1927.

When you get this,[1] you will probably think that I am married to a large lady, but it isn't quite so bad as that. It's all rather sad, but somehow I didn't have much to say about it—the invitations having been printed without my knowledge. I should have given more space to Mrs. Belmont, whom you will remember as Eleanor Robeson.

I hope you are much better by this time and that the ocean agrees with you. I sent a copy of Tristram to Gardiner, but will send along another to Bermuda to R.R.[2] There is going to be a lot of noise about it, and I only hope that it may survive—not to mention myself. Fortunately the New Hampshire woods are not far away.

My best wishes to you all.

TO MRS. LOUIS V. LEDOUX

Peterborough, August 20, 1927

This is not a very productive summer for me thus far, and I haven't much to say in reply to your letter except that otherwise I am doing very well, and still waiting for fifteen hundred pages of proof that should have been here long before now. You know, I believe, that my publishers are getting out a five volume set of my mighty works in the style of Tristram, which means a resetting of the whole business. They may as well be doing that as anything else, for I shall have no book for them this year. The well was pumped entirely dry last fall, and has simply got to fill up again. I managed to siphon up a sonnet for *McCall's* Magazine, for a large consideration, but don't yet know where it came from. It must be a pretty bad one. I have no good advice to give you except to read *The Canary Murder Mystery* and Ludwig's *Napoleon,* both of which are highly stimulating and very valuable. You might also be surprised to see how good *The Moonstone* still is. If your brain hasn't outgrown all such frivolity you had better try it.—I cannot make out from your letter that you are at all sorry, in any decent sense of the word, for R.'s six feet one of military misery. But I hope she will find the right fellow before long. I am getting a little old myself, going on fifty-eight, but I doubt if she would have me anyhow. I don't like jazz and I don't dance, and I don't take good care of my clothes —such as they are.—I had a note from Louis the other day, from which I inferred that he is still alive. I'm glad to know that, and this statement applies as well to you. Not long ago

I heard a morganatic marriage defined as chicken *à la King,* but I don't know whether that's really funny or not. I don't seem to know much of anything today.

TO JOSEPH FORD

Peterborough, September 5, 1927

While I appreciate fully your suggestion and your inducement, I have found it best to decline all invitations to read from my poems or public talks. I don't enjoy it, and don't do it well; and if such things are not done well, they had far better not be done at all as I know both as a performer and as a listener. Besides which, I have not been especially well this summer, and haven't done much work. If I hadn't been through the same thing before, it would be easy to imagine that I have written myself out, but there is really no such good news as that for those who insist that I have too much intellect. As a matter of fact, I haven't any just now or no more than is required to read the works of E. Phillips Oppenheim and Shakespeare. Today I don't know which is the greater. It is pleasant to hear from you again, and I thank you for your generous suggestion, even though I cannot act upon it.

TO LOUIS V. LEDOUX

Peterborough, September 28, 1927

I have just had to decline another invitation from the Frasers and I shall be doing you and Jean no more than a deed of mercy in staying away from you—for I'm really not fit for visiting, which requires, for pleasure on either side, that one should be in a better mood than I am now, after a summer that has produced hardly a single thought or image worth setting down. And everything has been made worse by a most infernal delay in getting the five volume edition going. But the proofs are coming at last and will keep me busy for some time. I shall stay in Boston until Thanksgiving or the first of December. New York keeps me going too much, and four or five months of it is about all I can manage. There is another book coming, but I doubt if it takes shape until next summer. After all, I have kept the wheels going steadily for the past seventeen years—even when I was wasting time on novels—and perhaps it isn't altogether surprising that I should have written myself out. There wasn't much left of me last fall, and anything like sustained work is only now taking on the shape of a possibility. My friends must—if they will—let me be the best judge of what is good for me, and not cuss me too hard if I seem at times a bit difficult and contrary. I owe everything to my friends already (and to a very few in particular) and so will take a debtor's advantage of asking a little more in the way of enduring my ways. They need never have any fear of my changing towards them.

TO NATHAN HASKELL DOLE

38 Ipswich Street, Boston
April 22, 1928

I wrote "scared years" when I was young, meaning something between bewildered and frightened. "Scarred" would go but it wouldn't mean what I had in mind.—Since then both words would have applied in one way or another to my years, which have piled up to fifty-eight; and I am still here by the grace of God.

I fled from New York to get away from "people" but I should be very glad to see you if you should find yourself in this part of the town. I should always be grateful to you as one of the first to find something in my work.

TO MRS. ALICE TILTON GARDIN [1]

Peterborough, June 21, 1928

All the dogs must be having a wonderful time with the whole state of Connecticut to run in, and I can see young Porgy going strong, ahead of all the others.

It is good to be young, especially for dogs, for they don't know enough—or perhaps they know too much—to look forward and see old age in the distance. I used to worry for fear of not living long enough, but now I worry, when I think of it, for fear of living too long. Apparently I was born not to be satisfied.

I saw Jimmy's pylon group in the Sunday *Times* and thought it came out rather well. In the course of time he will have monuments all over the country, and three or four thousand years from now people will have their casts and photographs of Frasers with broken arms and noses, just as we have the Venus of Milo and the three mysterious people from the pediment of the Acropolis, meaning to say Parthenon. I'm too intellectual now to send you any thrillers, but I have a rather good semi-highbrow novel that I'll send along in a few days. Pretty good, but not so nourishing as Edgar Wallace. Please remember me to everybody, even to the great-grandchild.

TO MRS. LOUIS V. LEDOUX

Peterborough, July 22, 1928

I hope you won't think from my delay in acknowledging your letter that I was not truthful in telling Louis that you would do a good deed in writing to me. Since receiving it I have written the greater part of another pleasant poem (about 1700 lines about a man who killed his wife because he wasn't altogether sure of her.[1]) The incident doesn't sound entirely new, but there are several ways of doing those things, and all sorts of reactions, varying with the temperature and the circumstances. Whenever I killed a wife, I used to be sorry and uncomfortable, and I have made this fellow rather wish he hadn't. But he is an awful egotist, and his uncertainty troubles him almost as much as his performance of extermination. It is instructive and highly moral. Having finished it in the rough, I had another idea and discovered that I could still write a short poem, which fills me with hope that I may write another book of them. Perhaps it isn't necessary that any more books by me should be written, but apparently I am so constructed that some bad habit or other is necessary for my existence, and books may be as harmless as any other.—A note from Torrence tells me that he is taking a cure at Geneva, but he doesn't know what for. He seems cheerful about it. Please write again when you will.

TO LEWIS M. ISAACS

Peterborough, July 27, 1928

I was wrong about the dedication in *C.C.* I remember now that Gardiner was so bewildered by the poem, which was pretty radical in those days, that I had not quite the heart to dedicate it to him as I had intended. But he came to think better of it before he died, and after his death I ventured to use his name. He was a good man, and I hope his ghost is not sorry for my well-meant acknowledgment.— I am very sorry to know that Mrs. Isaacs is still having so much trouble, and hope that something may be done soon to relieve her condition. . . . I know one man who was afflicted with an overpowering lassitude and uselessness that no doctor could account for until an expert found it all in his antrums, or antri, and made him lively as a flea again after a short treatment. In his case there was no rheumatism, so far as I know, but his experience shows that the removal of a local infection may work wonders.

My murderous poem [1] was done "pretty fast", but will need a considerable amount of going over. In the meantime I have written a short story [2] which I am sending along for you to have copied, if you will. You may keep the MS. and maybe buy a hat with it sometime.

I am almost inclined to say that Mrs. MacDowell is really better. At any rate, she has appeared so during the past two weeks.

Am I to see you here this summer? I hope so.

[Postscript]
Macmillan's statement just came.

$15,213.93
Poems for anthologies   157.50

15,371.43
Advance & mdse.   835.55

$14,535.88
which isn't so bad
for blank verse

Tristram   57,475 copies
$12,907.90
et cetera

TO LEWIS M. ISAACS

Peterborough, August 10, 1928

I am glad to have your letter and to know that Mrs. Isaacs appears to be on her way out of the woods. I hope surely that she will have no set-back—which isn't much of a word. If ever you find another puzzling place in any poem of mine, I wish you would let me know. Otherwise, it might possibly get by. Benét's book [1] was selected by the Book of the Month Club, which insured an immediate sale of 60,000 copies. He is a fortunate bard. I mind what you say of a trip abroad, but since my going dry, for physiological reasons, there appears to be nothing for me to do but to live it out as comfortably as possible, and with the fewest possible reminders of the world that was. A dry trip to Europe and to England would be an enormous annoyance, and one that I cannot even contemplate without horror and tears. New England is really the best place for me now. Chickens come home to roost. The rest of the country (excepting New York, where most of my friends are) means nothing to me, and I wouldn't give ten cents to see it. The Grand Canyon is no doubt a grand piece of work, but I know just about how it looks. I'm full of joy to know that you are likely to be here in September.

TO LOUIS V. LEDOUX

Boston, September 28, 1928

I don't know whether you want another book about me or not, but I'm sending one along (it would cost you five dollars)—also two others, which may one day be valuable. You are quite free to do with them as you like. Maybe you can read the Joyce thing.[1] I can't.

Jean tells me that you are all going around the world for a rest. Well, if that's your notion of resting, it just goes to show how differently we mortals are put together. For me, I should want for such a rest more than Brett owes me, which is more than fifteen thousand dollars—for some 58000 *Tristram*s, and other less popular works of *janius*. *Tristram*, by the way, is going over the radio next Tuesday evening in dramatic form with Wagner's music. God help us all— including Wagner, you will say. I'm pretty well done up after doing a year's work in a little over three months, and have been having a fuss with the limited edition of my *Sonnets*, which should have been out by this time. But at last they appear to be on the way. . . .

TO MRS. LAURA E. RICHARDS

Peterborough, June 19, 1929

This bottle of Higgins [1] must have friz last winter. Anyhow, all the snap and character have gone out of it. I'll have to get another. You are entirely wrong about my being steeped in Zola and Hardy when I was young. When I was young I read mostly Dickens, Dime Novels (which cost five cents), Elijah Kellogg, Harry Castleman, Oliver Optic, Horatio Alger, Bulwer-Lytton, Thackeray and Bryant's *Library of Poetry and Song*. When I wrote that rather pinfeatherish Zola sonnet I had read only *L'Assommoir*, and I have read only one of his books since then. I don't know the significance of the cromlech on the cover of *Cavender*, but the stars evidently mean that everything is crystal clear and has a happy ending.

We are having some powerful warm weather here.

TO MISS HELEN GRACE ADAMS [1]

328 East 42nd Street
January 1, 1930

In writing *Tristram* I was merely telling a story, using the merest outline of the old legend. Perhaps I should say adapting rather than using. There isn't much for you to write about it except in the way of general criticism. There is no symbolic significance in it, although there is a certain amount in *Merlin* and *Lancelot,* which were suggested by the world war—Camelot representing in a way the going of a world that is now pretty much gone. But possibly these two poems may be read just as well as narrative poems with no inner significance beyond that which is obvious. There is no "philosophy" in my poetry beyond an implication of an ordered universe and a sort of deterministic negation of the general futility that appears to be the basis of "rational" thought. So I suppose you will have to put me down as a mystic, if that means a man who cannot prove all his convictions to be true. I dislike "Rabbi Ben Ezra" so much as a poem that I haven't read it in something like thirty years, but I should say, not having a very clear memory of it, that its easy optimism is a reflection of temperament rather than of experience and observation. Those who do me the great honor of reading my books must excuse me from trying to interpret them—an occupation in which I should probably fail. If your thesis is printed I should be very glad to read it. This is a long letter for me to write about myself and may possibly be received by you as a dubious beginning of a New Year.

TO MRS. LAURA E. RICHARDS

328 East 42nd Street
February 2, 1930

Good heavings, no! "The House on the Hill" is no house
that ever was, and least of all a stone house still in good
order. I don't know why they assume and say such fool
things, but they do, and they will do so for evermore. They
will do so in heaven and they will do so in hell. Or, if necessary, they will do so in a condition of absolute annihilation.
Not even annihilation will cure them of that. . . . I am told
that a life of Lady Byron published last year is a master-
piece, altogether admirable and scandalous. You had better
read it and see if you like Lord George any better.

TO MRS. LOUIS V. LEDOUX

Peterborough, August 13, 1930

. . . I may as well tell you that my words are all used up.
They are all in the Long Thing¹ that I have been working
on since June tenth, and my head is so empty that it rings
like a brass kettle when I pound it in a frenzy. The new poem
is about a man who assumed that he was perfect until he
discovered that he wasn't. So you see it isn't autobiographi-
cal. It seems to me to "go", but my judgment in such matters
is not infallible and you had better not trust it altogether—
not that you would be likely to. *Nightingale*² sings in October, and Cestre's³ book on *E.A.R.* comes out in a few
days. . . . From what you have said, I rather think you will
like what the friendly Frenchman has to say about the Arthurian things. In fact he says a great deal that I have been
waiting for someone to say—not only praise, which in itself

doesn't always amount to much, but simple statements of what I have been trying to do. But you will judge for yourself as to that when you see the book. I realize now that my grist is in the time-mill and that there isn't much more for me to do about it. Sixty year old leopards cannot change their spots or their color. They can only change their teeth. . . . I am sorry for Louis in the city during the past month, which has been torrid enough even down here. There were days when I panted pentameters, but somehow they came, and I hope some of them are good. There are 2700 of them, and Louis had better guard against a squeaky throat before he tries to read them.

TO MRS. LAURA E. RICHARDS

Boston, November 15, 1930

I don't see how your article [1] on my brother could be better, and I can't begin to thank you properly for writing it. It really means a great deal to me. You will please remember that, and be sure that it would mean a great deal to him if he knew about it. Maybe he does, though I doubt it, and don't really wish to believe that whatever may be coming for us is to be shackled with memories of so scrappy a link of existence as this. Anyhow, we don't know much about the last one, which is probably better for us. If there wasn't any last one, I don't see how there can be a next one. But there are two or three other things that I don't see, and you must make allowances for the limited and unomniscient.

I trust that all goes well, and you don't say that it goes otherwise.

[Postscript]

I haven't disturbed what you say about me. You may call me names, if you like. No (final) "e" in Dean.

TO PERCY MACKAYE

Peterborough, September 15, 1931

It is good news indeed that you have Robin[1] with you again, and it must be the best of all possible news for him. I hope most sincerely that everything will go better for you all from now on.—As for my letters, you and Ford may do with them as you think best. There cannot be anything in them of a very startling—or, I fear very valuable—nature; and I will trust both of you not to include anything that your instinct tells you might make me squirm in my grave. I doubt if a book of my letters would be of much general interest, but a book of selections from them might be readable and possibly mildly amusing. I don't know about that, for I don't remember anything that is in them. In the meantime I appreciate greatly the interest that you and Ford, and a few others, have always taken in my work.

TO DR. WILL DURANT

Peterborough, September 18, 1931

I have delayed my acknowledgment of your letter only for the lack of anything especially profound or valuable to say in reply to it. I told a philosopher once that all the other philosophers would have to go out of business if one of them should happen to discover the truth; and now you say, or imply, in your letter that the truth has been discovered, and that we are only the worse off, if possible, for the discovery. This is naturally a cause of some chagrin and humiliation for me, for I had heard nothing about it. It is true that we have acquired a great deal of material knowledge in recent years, but so far as knowledge of the truth itself is concerned, I cannot see that we are any nearer to it now than our less imaginative ancestors were when they cracked each others' skulls with stone hatchets, or that we know any more than they knew of what happened to the soul that escaped in the process. It is easy, and just now rather fashionable, to say that there is no soul, but we do not know whether there is a soul or not. If a man is a materialist, or a mechanist, or whatever he likes to call himself, I can see for him no escape from belief in a futility so prolonged and complicated and diabolical and preposterous as to be worse than absurd; and as I do not know that such a tragic absurdity is not a fact, I can only know my native inability to believe that it is one. There is nothing in the thought of annihilation that frightens me; for it would be, at the worst, nothing more terrible than going to sleep at the end of a long day, whether a pleasant or a painful one, or both. But if life is only what it appears to be, no amount of improvement or enlightenment will ever compensate or atone for what it has inflicted and endured in ages past, or for what it is inflicting and enduring today. Only the most self-centred and short-visioned of egoists, it seems to me, will attempt to deny the truth of a statement so obvious, though I am aware that its obviousness is no warrant for our wasting much time over it. Our teleological endowment spares most of us from worrying over such matters to any great extent, or from disturbing ourselves unduly over the freedom of the will. There is apparently not much that anyone can do about it except to follow his own light—which may or may not be the light of an *ignis fatuus* in a swamp. The cocksureness of the modern "mechanist" means nothing to me; and I doubt if it means any more to him when he pauses really to think. His position is not entirely unlike that of an intrepid explorer standing on a promontory in a fog, looking through the newest thing in the way of glasses for an ocean that he cannot see, and shouting to his mechanistic friends behind him that he has found the end of the world.

These remarks, which to some readers might seem a little severe, are more the result of observation and reflection than of personal discomfort or dissatisfaction. As lives go, my own life would be called, and properly, a rather fortunate one.

TO MRS. RIDGELY TORRENCE

Boston, November 4, 1931

. . . As for *Matthias,* you don't have to read him again. I just wanted to be sure that he hadn't gone astray. So far as I can make out, people seem to like him.

The enclosed letter [1] to the London *Times* may interest you as a Proustite. I have always considered the first two hundred pages or so of *Dombey and Son* about the best of Dickens—leaving out the death-bed scene, in which he slopped over entirely. All the rest of the Paul part is unapproachable—which doesn't mean anything, except that there is nothing else like it.

I shall be in New York sometime in December.

TO MISS BESS DWORSKY

Boston, December 7, 1931

I am naturally gratified to learn that you are writing a thesis on my poetry, but I am rather sorry to learn that you are writing about my "philosophy"—which is mostly a statement of my inability to accept a mechanistic interpretation of the universe and of life. As I see it, my poetry is not pessimistic, nothing of an infinite nature can be proven or disproven in finite terms—meaning words—and the rest is probably a matter of one's individual ways of seeing and feeling things. There is no sense in saying that this world is not a pretty difficult place, but that isn't pessimism. The real pessimist sees too much of one thing, and the optimist is too likely to see only what he wishes to see—or perhaps not to see at all beyond the end of his famous nose. I still wish that you were writing about my poetry—of which my so-called philosophy is only a small part, and probably the least important. . . .

TO MRS. LAURA E. RICHARDS

328 East 42nd Street
January 10, 1932

I am pleased that you seem to like *Sisera*. All the nice ladies who have read it seem to like it. There must be something in it that appeals to the feminine heart. I have just been reading Seward's life of *George Meredith,* and still cannot like the man. Something that I haven't liked has always leaked out through the cracks in his work. Maybe you have felt it, maybe not. I haven't yet tackled *Paradise Lost,* but I'm going to. The last Oppenheim led me astray. "O, pity and shame, that they who to live well entend so fair, should turn aside to tread Paths indirect, or in the midway faint."

TO MRS. LAURA E. RICHARDS

328 East 42nd Street
January 18, 1932

You are surely right in your objection to "hight" as Miss Millay uses it. But what can I do about it? She has never asked me for advice, and somehow I suspect that she never will. Her last book is a most remarkable business, and yet it seems to me in some way more literary than alive. For some reason I haven't gone back to it. "If and when" I do, I may change my mind. All the same, she is an eminent little critter, and deserves to be eminent. What do you think of Elinor Wylie? She is to John Donne what The Millay is to Shakespeare—if you care to figure that out. . . .

TO MRS. LAURA E. RICHARDS

328 East 42nd Street
February 3, 1932

I suppose you have heard *Norma*, which has lately been revived and is going strong. I know a good many of the tunes, in the nature of things, and so enjoyed them all the more. In fact, I had a grand good time—which isn't so easy after one gets to 62 1/6, and has been dry for nearly seven years. If people should stop buying blank verse, there would be nothing left for me but that poorhouse, which you told me had burned down. So there wouldn't be even that. The Lord only knows what there would be—or what there will be anyhow for any of us, from the looks of this world. On the whole, and all things considered, I'm rather glad—bein' as I am—that I'm not beginning at the other end. All the same, I am glad to have known you.

Your obedient minstrel
E.A.R.

TO MRS. LAURA E. RICHARDS

Peterborough, August 31, 1932

The eclipse must have got hold of me today, for I haven't been able to do anything except to read parts of *King Lear*. There is no sense in writing things like that, for after reading it a fellow sees no sense in his writing at all. It is nearly all language—but Lord, what language. *Hamlet,* on the other hand, is language and character—and something else that no one has ever found a name for. The Baby[1] is due in about two weeks, and will be a boy with a loud voice. But not too loud—so you needn't be scared. . . . I have nothing in especial to lament—excepting always a misspent life.

TO MRS. LOUIS V. LEDOUX

Peterborough, September 28, 1932

. . . I have been grinding at the mill all summer and have a sack of something or other to show for it. The grist this time is a little different—not so heavy, and not at all bitter. Of course I am never really bitter, or anything but cheerful and full of metaphysical joy and hope, but people don't seem to understand that and so call me all sorts of names which also they don't understand. So far as I can make out, most people are so afraid of life that when they see it coming their first impulse is to get behind a tree and shut their eyes. And for some odd reason they call that impulse optimism—which has always seemed funny to me.—This new poem is a sort of narrative comedy in blank verse, and will probably make Louis tear out handfuls of his hair. If these modern long things of mine survive their first hundred years, which are said to be the hardest, they may go on longer. Anyhow, I had to do them. . . .

TO MRS. LAURA E. RICHARDS

328 East 42nd Street
January 20, 1933

I don't remember making any such remark about the churches, but if you say I made it, I can only say that you are, to the best of my belief, generally speaking, a truthful lady. At the worst, it couldn't have been anything more than one of my easy exaggerations, which aren't supposed to be taken literally. But of course they are, and so make a lot of trouble for me—like many lines of mine that aren't supposed to bring tears. On the other hand, I'm not so sure that my prophecy was altogether a wrong one. Leaving out the Romans and the Methodists, there doesn't seem to be much left of the churches but the buildings. Even the Romans will have to contrive some sort of symbolic compromise before long; and as for the Methodists, who come nearer to ruling us than we suspect, they are perhaps more an incorporated and shrewdly organized Ignorance than they are a church, and the Church of England is more like a social club, with music and trimmings, than like anything in the Scriptures. The Christian theology has so thoroughly crumbled that I do not think of any non-Roman acquaintance to whom it means anything—and I doubt if you do. The Christian ethics might have done some good if they had ever been tried, or understood, but I'm afraid it's too late now. There's a non-theological religion on the way, probably to be revealed by science when science comes definitely to the jumping-off place. It is really there now, but isn't quite ready to say so.

This is a beautiful day, but a little too warm for the season. It's always an imperfect world.

TO MRS. LAURA E. RICHARDS

328 East 42nd Street
February 13, 1933

I am always impressed by a picture of Bishop ———, who looks as if he had been brought up by the devil—though

I don't suppose he was exactly. Did you happen to see an article about him a few years ago in *Harper's* Magazine? . . . It is almost worth your sending someone to rummage the Public Library for your entertainment, or Mr. Richards's. Bishop Potter used to say that it was his business to teach his shepherds how to tend their flocks, implying that he was free to climb fences and enjoy the scenery in his own way. Now his effigy lies horizontal in the Cathedral of Saint John the Divine. Blessed are the meek. —As for religion in the future, I didn't say that it wouldn't be mystical. Of course it must be that in order to be a religion, but it will be free of all theological machinery. I suppose you know about the recusant gentleman who said that he might believe in the Trinity when he saw one man riding in three carriages.—Mr. Pennington of Golder's Green is to be commended for his good taste.—I heard the *Rheingold,* but not the *Valkyrie,* and I heard *The Emperor Jones* out of curiosity—and because I know the composer. I came away rather glad that Wagner was permitted to live. You may be interested to know I find him greater and more incredible as time goes on. He may have been a bounder, but he couldn't have bounded all the time. . . .

TO MRS. LAURA E. RICHARDS

328 East 42nd Street
March 3, 1933

You know of course that Mrs. Perry has gone—very quietly, after only twenty-four hours of illness. One can only say nothing is here for tears, for she really wanted to go, and had, apparently, an absolute faith in meeting her friends. I doubt if she meets them, but I don't know that she will not. My notion of immortality, and I have some sort of notion, doesn't include the memory of this rather trivial—and for most people much worse than that—phase of existence. A clumsy sentence, but never mind.—If I had remembered your birthday (I never remember anybody's, and sometimes not even my own) I should have written something nice and pleasant and friendly. So you will please consider it as written and received, with my wish that both you and Mr. Richards will have many more. There is every reason why you should have them. Poor Mrs. Perry was almost entirely alone, and was angry with Time for taking away her strength and leaving her in other ways as young as ever. She could have fallen wildly in love again if the right sort of brisk young fellow had come along. Speaking of love, and such like, I'll go down stairs now and hear some *Tristan* over the radio. Are you hearing it? *Death Answers the Bell*[1] is a good Valentine Williams. I read *The Frightened Lady*[2], but have forgotten what it was about, though I've a dim notion that it was good.

TO LEWIS M. ISAACS

Peterborough, August 10, 1933

The depression shows itself in my publisher's statement to April 30—$4346—which is probably better than some writers of blank verse have done. They sold 7444 *Nicodemuses*—which might also be worse. There's a bad slump in the *Collected Poems*—723 copies. But this may not be surprising, as most people who like poetry haven't got five dollars. *Tristram* goes along—1846 copies. It looks as if I should be able to live through another year—though my last one cost me $7000 in some way or other. Going dry doesn't settle everything.

There is to be a limited edition of *Talifer*—they say between 250 and 300 copies, which shows that there are still a few who aren't entirely broke.—I am three-quarters through my nightmare poem [1], and everything is going better now that I have had an ulcerated jaw-tooth out. . . .

TO HERMANN HAGEDORN

Peterborough, September 17, 1933

I am glad to know that you are on this side of the ocean again, and from what I hear of the other side, I rather fancy that you are not sorry. It is good too to know that you have a light, for without one a fellow is either comfortably blind or wretchedly astray. I have always had one to keep me going, though I fear that you and several others have thought at times that it was burning pretty low. Maybe it was, but it never went out, and I think there is oil enough in it to last me for the rest of my journey—which can't be a very long one now. But even at sixty-four I don't think much about that.—I have just finished another long poem, this time a sort of nightmare about people who are living in the wrong world. I don't think of anything just like it, and I don't think it is altogether bad. Anyhow, I hope it isn't. I'll be sending along my cheerful one, written last summer, in a few days. No murders or suicides in it.

My best wishes to you all, as always.

TO MRS. MABEL DODGE LUHAN

Boston, November 15, 1933

Please observe the merciful pencil again—which is bad form but good humanity. I don't want to destroy your eyes, for you will need them now and then.

I have read the *Memoirs* with all the interest that you could ask, and I can see nothing the matter with them as a piece of writing. The only question is that of publication, and here I have to hesitate. You don't ask for suggestions, but somehow I fancy that you will expect some sort of comment along that line. So I'll say frankly that I think the publication of the *Memoirs* during your life, or during the lives of several people who are involved, would be a great mistake, and one that you would regret. About all that I can suggest is that you put it away for publication say twenty years after your death—which, I trust, is a long time distant. If ever it is published, the "sikes" will probably call you long names, like "exhibitionist" perhaps, but when you are gone you will not mind a little thing like that. You were wise in not listening to editors and publishers, who wanted of course to make money, regardless of your position or of other people's feelings. I'm not referring now to myself, for what you say about me is at the worst, and only in a few places, perhaps a little annoying. Most of it is either amusing or complimentary, or both—though I'm sorry that you find my poetry so uninteresting. But those things are beyond our control, and I don't hold your opinions against you. I have difficulty with poets who are far more famous than I shall ever be.—So I'll say, for the lack of something more specific, that your memoirs are amazingly well done and altogether interesting—to put it mildly. Your own judgment and reflection will have to tell you what is to become of them.

I am returning them with many thanks, and with much appreciation of your compliment to me in sending them. Will you please send me a word to let me know that you have received them?

TO CRAVEN LANGSTROTH BETTS

328 East 42nd Street
January 3, 1934

I am sorry to know that Mrs. Betts has been having such an unhappy time, and in spite of all you say I suspect that you haven't any too much to go on just now. So I'm sending another enclosure—not a very large one—to meet any immediate convalescent requirements. She may want a guinea-hen or something—or a bottle of fizzy wine, or perchance a bottle of good whiskey, if such a thing is to be had. Anyhow, please ask her, with my compliments, to get something that she does want.—The critics wrote so much foolishness about *Talifer* that they appear to have done little harm, except perhaps in and about New York. It is going about the same as *Nicodemus,* which is all I expected. Of course the times make a difference, and maybe I'd better not try again to be cheerful. Straighten out your back night and morning against lumbago.

TO HOUSTON MARTIN

328 East 42nd Street
January 12, 1934

In reply to your very kind letter of the sixth—I will say that there seems to me to be no question as to the enduring quality of A. E. Housman's poetry. I do not think of any living writer whose work is likely to live longer—if as long. For some reason I find it difficult to select the two or three of his poems that I like best, and this may be the highest compliment that I can pay to his work.

I am rather surprised that you should have heard so much

commendation of my work from English writers. With a few exceptions, they have maintained—or I supposed they had—a rather too consistent national reticence in regard to it. And I still doubt if many of them are familiar with it. . . .

TO MRS. LAURA E. RICHARDS

328 East 42nd Street
February 12, 1934

Abraham Lincoln liked "Oh, why should the spirit of mortal be proud," because it made him think of what poor critters we are. Today I have been thinking of Hitler, and of what one neurotic fanatic may yet do to us and drag us into. It's all right to say it can't happen, but unfortunately it can. The more I try to make a picture of this world for the next hundred years, the more I don't like it, and the gladder I am that I shall be out of it. But something better will come sometime, we'll hope, in spite of human stupidity, which is a large part of destiny. . . .

[Postscript]
Spectators received.

TO MOWRY SABEN

328 East 42nd Street
February 22, 1934

I don't know what George Washington would think of his country if he could come back to it now, and I'm afraid he couldn't tell us much more about it, or where it is going, than we know today. If there isn't a war in Europe—which means, if Hitler isn't quite sure that he can gobble Austria or Poland at this time—I think we'll get along somehow. There is a lot of untried resource and vitality in this country that will require a lot of smothering before we hear its death-squeak. . . .

TO ARCHIBALD MACLEISH

257 West Newton Street, Boston
April 12, 1934

Dr. Merrill Moore left with me the other day his copy of your *Collected Poems*, which I have been reading with a great deal of satisfaction and admiration. I had already read *Conquistador*, and had admired it as something extremely different from anything else. But for some reason, or for no reason, had seen only a few of your shorter things. You are tired of hearing praise of "You, Andrew Marvell", but I fear that you cannot keep people from praising it, all the same. It is really a magical thing. And the whole book is one to make a fellow sit up and be glad.

I hope you won't mind this unsolicited word of congratulation from a stranger who has usually to do the best he can with words that are solicited.

TO W. H. GERRY

257 West Newton Street
April 9, 1934

I am glad to tide you over a bad spot, and only wish it were possible for me to be of some really substantial service. But there are so many demands on me now that I can't do more than this at present. Don't think of paying it back—

or not until you can do it without any trouble. I never give advice to poets (except not to be in a hurry to publish) but sometimes I wonder if mere "writing" isn't in ninety-nine cases in a hundred about the worst sort of a dog's life. If you could get something entirely different to do for the next ten years, you would then be still young for the writing of a novel of any probable importance. Unless a man is a boiling over genius of the first order, like Dickens, he is not likely to have a real novel in him before he is forty—and only a few have it then. Please don't be offended, for I'm only telling you indirectly that I don't want you to starve.

TO MRS. LAURA E. RICHARDS

Peterborough, September 11, 1934

. . . You may just possibly be interested to know that I have nearly come to the conclusion that a daddy-long-legs has about the meanest deal of anything in nature—excepting possibly an elk with his heavy horns. I'm afraid, on the whole, that there isn't much comfort in nature as a visible evidence of God's infinite love. It appears to be a shambles and a torture-chamber from the insects up—or should we say down? The insects will have the world some day, and maybe they'll eat everything that's on it, and then eat each other. For some reason or other this makes me think of an epitaph by Thomas Hardy. You may know it?

> *"I'm Smith of Stoke. Aged sixty-odd,*
> *I've lived without a dame*
> *From youth-time on; and would to God*
> *My dad had done the same."*

I don't hear Meredith mentioned nowadays, but Henry James is still going strong in his always limited way. Mere-

1. Virgil, *Eclogue III*, "Palaemon." Copied and revised solely for the delectation of A. R. Gledhill.

Palaemon—Damoetas—Menalcas

Menalcas.
Whose flock is that, Damoetas? Meliboeus'?

Damoetas.
No, Argon lately placed them in my care.

M.
O sheep! forever an unhappy flock!
While, fearful of my own supremacy,
Argon himself the fair Naera courts,
The guard Damoetas drains them twice an hour
And robs the lambs and mothers of their milk.

D.
Less freedom, sir, in dealing words to men;
For well we know both who corrupted you
And what the goats with sidelong glances saw;
And more, we know the cave wherein 'twas done—
The kindly Dryads laughing all the while.
("And the good-natured Nymphs etc.")

M.
And doubtless, too, they saw me with my knife
To cut the vines and tender shoots of Ulycon.

D.
Or rather when amidst this ancient wood
You broke the arrows and the bow of Daphne's
Which you, Menalcas, grieved to see returned
And would have died but for the pain you gave him.

M.
Where are the masters while their raging slaves
Dare to address me thus! O wicked one,
Did I not see you trap the goat of Damon,
Lycisca barking madly all the time?
And when I called out, "Tityrus, where goes he?
Collect your flock!"—you hid amid the sedge.

D.
And should he not yield up the goat to me,
Since with my voice and reed I conquered him?
If you would know it, sir, the goat is mine:
Damon himself confessed as much to me,
Yet says he cannot pay one what is due.

181

M.

You won a prize at singing! as if you
Could play a waxen reed! Why clown, 'tis yours
To blow your murderous note upon the highway.

D.

Lo! shall we have a contest here between us?
I'll stake this heifer, and, lest you refuse
I'll say she comes to milking twice a day,
And feeds two calves besides. Now, my good friend,
What pawn will you advance to cover mine?

M.

I dare not meet thy wager from the flock:
My father is at home, and worse than that,
A crabbed step-dame: both count twice a day
The sheep, and one the kids. But I will pledge—
Since 'tis your will to carry out this folly—
What you yourself will own far worthier:
These beechen cups wrought by Alcimedon
On which the ivy, exquisitely carved
With facile chisel, sweetly intermingles
Its scattered fruit and pallid foliage.
Two figures are engravéd in the center:
The one is Conon, and—who was the other?—
Who with his rod marks out the world for man—
The time for ploughing and for harvesting?
These are kept hidden; lips have never touched them.

D.

Alcimedon has made for me two bowls
And wound the handles round with acanthus;
With Orpheus graven in a woodland scene.
These two are hidden; lips have never touched them.
Yet if you will but look upon my heifer
The cups are nothing to deserve your praise.

M.

Let there be no delay, for I will come
Wherever you may call. Or let the one
Who now approaches hear us—look—Palaemon.
And I will take good care that in the future
Damoetas tortures no man with his voice.

D.

Begin, if you have anything to sing;
You'll find me ready, nor will I dispute
The judgment; therefore, my good friend Palaemon,
I pray you balance well within your mind
This contest; 'tis no trifling affair.

Palaemon

Sing, as we sit amid the tufted grass:
Now all the field and all the wood is blooming;
The trees are green, the year is in its glory,
Begin, Damoetas, and Menalcas follow;
Alternately—the way the muses love.

D.

Begin with Jove, O Ulysses! all things are full of Jove:
'Tis he that loves the earth; 'tis he that loves my song.

M.

Phoebus loves me: for him I ever keep close by
His chosen gifts; the laurel and blushing hyacinth.

D.

Galatea, playful maiden, seeks me with an apple;
Then flies, but wishes to be seen before she hides.

M.

My flame Amyntas comes of his own will to me,
And Delia to my dogs is now no better known.

D.

I'll make my love a gift: for I have found the spot
Where the high-soaring pigeons rear their tender young.

M.

I've sent my love ten apples all ruddy from the woodland—
As many as I could: I'll send ten more tomorrow.

D.

How many and how sweet the words of Galatea!
Bear them aloft ye winds, so may th'immortals hear them.

M.

Where is my joy, although you hold me dear, Amyntas,
While you pursue the goats for me to tend the toils?

D.

Bid Phyllis come to me, Iolas; 'tis my birthday.
I offer sacrifice ere long; then you may come.

M.

But I love Phyllis more: she weeps at separation;
And cries "Farewell! Farewell! a long farewell!"—Iolas.

D.

Wolves to the flock are fatal; showers to ripened grain;
Wind to the trees; to me the wrath of Amaryllis.

M.

Rain cheers the crops; arbutus is sweet to tender kids;
Osier to laden sheep, to me none save Amyntas.

D.

Great Pollis loves to hear the rustic song I sing;
O, mountain Muses, rear a heifer to your lover.

M.

He writes a wondrous song—Oh, feed the bull that now
Lifts high his head and spurns the sand beneath his feet.

D.

Who loves thee, Pollis, may win thy cherished fame:
For him may honey flow and bramble bear amomum.

M.

Who hates not Bavius must love thy song, O Maevius!
And he would milk a butting goat, or yoke his foxes.

D.

O boys, who gather flowers and growing fruits of earth,
Flee hence!—a long cold snake is lying in the grass.

M.

My sheep, go not too near! you cannot trust the bank;
For even now the rain shakes out his dripping fleece.

D.

O Tityrus, from the stream call back your feeding flock:
Ere long I'll wash them all myself, in yonder spring.

M.

O boys, collect the sheep—if summer's burning heat,
As formerly, destroys the milk we work in vain.

D.

Alas! how lank and lean my bull stands in the field!
The love that kills the herd will kill the keeper too.

M.

But love is not in mine—their bones scarce held together:
I cannot tell the eye that charms my tender lambs.

D.

Oh, tell me in what land, and be my great Apollo,
Only three ells of sky lie open to the sight.

M.

Oh, tell me in what land the written names of kings
Are born with blooming flowers and Phyllis shall be thine.

Pal.

'Tis not for me to judge so fine a matter;
The prize belongs to one as to the other:
To any one who sings of love so sweet,
Or labors through such sorrow.—Now, my boys,
The rivers close—the fields have drunk their fill.

Nov. 1889

2. Mr. Gledhill's fiancée was a singer.

JULY 14, 1899 (MASON)

1. Philip Henry Savage (1868–1899), poet and Harvard acquaintance of E. A. R.

2. *Captain Craig.*

AUGUST 27, 1899 (MASON)

1. *Captain Craig.*

NOTES

SEPTEMBER 7, 1899 (MASON)

1. The "Author's Preface" to *Silex Scintillans or Sacred Poems* by Henry Vaughan.
2. "The Gypsy Trail."

OCTOBER 30, 1899 (MASON)

1. The reference is to E. A. R.'s own partial deafness.

MARCH 25, 1900 (GARDINER)

1. A member of the publishing firm of the same name.
2. E. A. R. had been employed for a time, in a minor position, in the administrative offices of Harvard University.

APRIL 18, 1900 (MASON)

1. "An Ode in Time of Hesitation."

NOVEMBER 25, 1900 (MISS PEABODY)

1. *Captain Craig.*
2. An Indian chief referred to in *Captain Craig.*
3. Small, Maynard & Co.
4. *The Masque of Judgment* by William Vaughn Moody.

DECEMBER 25, 1900 (MASON)

1. *The Poems of Philip Henry Savage,* edited with an introduction by Daniel Gregory Mason.

JANUARY 1, 1901 (MISS PEABODY)

1. Edmund Clarence Stedman's reference to Swedenborg's statement that the angels continually grow younger.
2. Fullerton Waldo, a Harvard contemporary and friend.

JANUARY 17, 1901 (GARDINER)

1. *A Literary History of America* by Barrett Wendell. Charles Scribner's Sons, 1900.

JANUARY 30, 1901 (MISS PEABODY)

1. Lawrence J. Henderson, then a student in Harvard Medical School, now a professor there.

APRIL 12, 1901 (MISS PEABODY)

1. "Isaac and Archibald."
2. "The Book of Annandale."
3. Seth Ellis Pope, a friend of E. A. R.'s from boyhood.
4. Edmund Clarence Stedman, the poet.
5. *Marlowe.*

JUNE 25, 1901 (MISS PEABODY)

1. Joseph Ford, a Harvard friend.
2. Mrs. Richard Henry Stoddard, wife of the poet.
3. William Vaughn Moody's *Masque of Judgment.*

SEPTEMBER 26, 1901 (MASON)

1. The American public.
2. At many times in his life, E. A. R. spoke of New Zealand as a foreign country that he would particularly care to visit.

JANUARY 18, 1902 (MRS. RICHARDS)

1. A discarded poem.
2. "The Klondike."
3. "The Wilderness."
4. The volume containing "Captain Craig."
5. William Vaughn Moody.
6. *Cf.* an anecdote related by Mr. Edwin Stringham, to the effect that E. A. R., during one of his last summers at the MacDowell Colony, once replied to some young colonists who spoke of his work as done in blacks and grays: "Those are the colors that last."

FEBRUARY 1902 (MRS. RICHARDS)

1. The shorter poems, which he had planned to publish separately from *Captain Craig*—L.E.R.
2. "The Woman and the Wife."

JANUARY 23, 1904 (MISS PEABODY)

1. Editor of the *Critic*.
2. Daniel Gregory Mason.
3. Editors of *The Outlook*.

JANUARY 26, 1905 (MISS PEABODY)

1. Miss Peabody had written a letter of protest to George Bernard Shaw, on the publication of *Man and Superman*.

APRIL 11, 1905 (GILDER)

1. E. A. R. was at that time employed in the advertising department of the Boston department store belonging to the father of his Harvard friend, William Edward Butler.

(UNDATED) 1905 (MRS. RICHARDS)

1. E. A. R.'s Custom House job, to which he had lately been appointed by President Theodore Roosevelt.

JULY 22, 1908 (MASON)

1. George Burnham, a friend from Harvard days.

JULY 20, 1910 (L. LEDOUX)

1. The reference is to "Vickery's Mountain" by E. A. R.

JULY 29, 1910 (MRS. MOODY)

1. Mr. T. H. Bartlett, sculptor, and father of the sculptor Paul Bartlett.

AUGUST 20, 1910 (L. LEDOUX)

1. The quotation is from Butcher and Lang's translation of *The Odyssey*, Book IX, lines 103 and 104.

OCTOBER 17, 1910 (MACKAYE)
1. William Vaughn Moody died October 17, 1910, at Colorado Springs.

AUGUST 14, 1911 (L. LEDOUX)
1. May Sinclair, the novelist.
2. A poem by George Edward Woodberry.

AUGUST 27, 1911 (MRS. MOODY)
1. "The Death of Eve."

SEPTEMBER 18, 1912 (HAGEDORN)
1. Mrs. Clara Potter Davidge, in whose homes (in New York and at La Tourette, Richmond, Staten Island) E. A. R. lived during the greater part of the time from 1909 to 1913.
2. Henry Fitch Taylor, the painter, whom Mrs. Davidge later married.

MARCH 7, 1913 (ISAACS)
1. Winthrop Ames.

MARCH 9, 1913 (GARDINER)
1. Alfred Henry Noyes, English poet.

DECEMBER 15, 1913 (HAGEDORN)
1. A reference to E. A. R.'s poem "The Field of Glory."

FEBRUARY 3, 1914 (MRS. MARKS)
1. *The Wolf of Gubbio,* by Josephine Preston Peabody.

AUGUST 10, 1914 (MRS. LEDOUX)
1. Albert R. Ledoux, the father-in-law of E. A. R.'s correspondent, usually was called Dr. Ledoux, but he was a Doctor of Philosophy, not a physician.
2. "The Mutt" was an Airedale.

JUNE 28, 1915 (K. ROOSEVELT)
1. A speech of Otto Mink, a character in *Van Zorn,* the play by E. A. R.
2. *The Porcupine.*
3. *The Man Against the Sky.*

DECEMBER 10, 1915 (MRS. MOODY)
1. *A History of English Literature,* by William Vaughn Moody and Robert Morss Lovett, published by Scribners.

MARCH 2, 1916 (DR. LEDOUX)
1. *The Man Against the Sky.*

JUNE 1, 1916 (HAGEDORN)
1. "Genevieve and Alexandra."

JULY 30, 1916 (MRS. LEDOUX) .

1. George P. Brett, Sr., President of The Macmillan Company.

AUGUST 14, 1916 (MRS. LEDOUX)

1. Lila Cabot Perry (Mrs. Thomas Sergeant Perry).

JULY 11, 1917 (L. N. CHASE)

1. Lewis Nathaniel Chase, a professor of English.

AUGUST 25, 1917 (ISAACS)

1. *Lancelot.*

OCTOBER 23, 1919 (ISAACS)

1. The amount of a prize, offered by Samuel Roth for a poem, won by *Lancelot.*

DECEMBER 24, 1919 (MACKAYE)

1. A symposium, for E. A. R.'s fiftieth birthday, of appreciations of his work. The symposium was conceived and organized by Percy Mac-Kaye, who arranged for its publication in the *New York Times* in December 1919.

2. *E. A.—a Milestone for America,* an article by Percy MacKaye in the *North American Review,* December 1919.

JANUARY 18, 1920 (MISS B. ROBINSON)

1. His niece, now Mrs. Harold Holt, of Urbana, Ill.

2. Both Mrs. Nivison and Mrs. Legg felt great enthusiasm for their work in Labrador under Dr. Wilfred Grenfell.

3. Ruth Robinson, another niece, now Mrs. William Nivison.

4. Marie Robinson, a third niece, later Mrs. Arthur T. Legg.

MAY 12, 1921 (MISS AMY LOWELL)

1. Copy of the clipping referred to:

THE KINDLY ARLINGTON

(From the *Cleveland Plain Dealer*)

"Speaking of Amy Lowell's verse, the other day, Edwin Arlington Robin-son said: 'Some of it would make good material for real poetry.'

"That's what we like about Brother Arl—He's so good-hearted that he can always find something good in everything."

OCTOBER 14, 1921 (BYNNER)

1. "Mr. Flood's Party."

DECEMBER 16, 1921 (R. TORRENCE)

1. E. A. R.'s *Collected Poems.*

FEBRUARY 3, 1922 (DRINKWATER)

1. Mr. and Mrs. St. John Ervine.

MAY 18, 1923 (MISS R. RICHARDS)

1. *Roman Bartholow.*
2. *Oaklands,* the home of the Gardiner family.

JUNE 2, 1924 (MRS. RICHARDS)

1. The life of Shelley by André Maurois.

JULY 11, 1924 (MRS. RICHARDS)

1. Author of a small volume of poems called *Clio,* which was published in 1924 by Blackwell.

JULY 31, 1924 (MRS. RICHARDS)

1. Dr. Alanson Tucker Schumann, poet and physician, Robinson's earliest literary friend.
2. The reference is to the death of Mrs. Richards's eldest daughter Alice.

MAY 11, 1925 (TORRENCE)

1. *Dionysus in Doubt* had received the Pulitzer Prize.

JUNE 26, 1925 (ISAACS)

1. Miss Marian Isaacs took part in a dramatic performance at Radcliffe.

AUGUST 3, 1926 (MISS BATES)

1. In reply to my praising Morgan Le Fay's letter, and also asking how Tristan and Isolt happened to be at Joyous Gard.—E.W.B.

APRIL 30, 1927 (MRS. RICHARDS)

1. A ticket was enclosed, admitting two to the Little Theatre, for an evening in honor of Edwin Arlington Robinson; a reading from *Tristram* by Mrs. August Belmont.
2. Miss Rosalind Richards.

JUNE 21, 1928 (MRS. GARDIN)

1. Mother of Mrs. James Earle Fraser.

JULY 22, 1928 (MRS. LEDOUX)

1. *Cavender's House.*

JULY 27, 1928 (ISAACS)

1. *Cavender's House.*
2. "Hector Kane," a poem.

AUGUST 10, 1928 (ISAACS)

1. *John Brown's Body,* by Stephen Vincent Benét.

SEPTEMBER 28, 1928 (L. LEDOUX)

1. *Anna Livia Plurabelle,* by James Joyce.

JUNE 19, 1929 (MRS. RICHARDS)

1. Ink.

1. In preparing a thesis for a Master's degree, Miss Adams had written to E. A. R., asking for a statement in regard to his "theory of poetry and philosophy of life in general."

AUGUST 13, 1930 (MRS. LEDOUX)

1. *Matthias at the Door.*
2. *The Glory of the Nightingales.*
3. *An Introduction to Edwin Arlington Robinson,* by Charles Cestre. Macmillan, 1930.

NOVEMBER 15, 1930 (MRS. RICHARDS)

1. He refers to the following article by Mrs. Richards. It was published in the Kennebec *Journal*.

HORACE DEAN ROBINSON

On hearing that Edwin Arlington Robinson had given one thousand dollars to the Gardiner Hospital as a memorial to his brother, the late Dr. Horace Dean Robinson, the friends of the hospital were deeply moved. It was not only the generosity of the gift, though that was notable; several other factors seemed to give it a special significance.

It shows that with faithful and loyal natures, time and absence have little power over Memory; shows, too, that loving Memory may be an actual and living force for good in any community. Those of his own and the elder generation remember Dean Robinson well; and now that his brother's gift has brought him back to dwell among us as what he longed to be, a helper and healer, let us try briefly to recall the man as he lived.

Horace Dean Robinson was born in Alna, Maine, May 30th, 1857, being the eldest son of Edward and Mary E. (Palmer) Robinson. He came to Gardiner with his parents in 1870; went through the Gardiner High School and the Maine Medical School, then a part of Bowdoin College; and thereafter took up the practice of his profession in Gardiner. He was elected City Physician in 1882, for the year 1882-3. In 1884 he moved to Camden, Maine, and practised his profession there for several years, returning to Gardiner in 1889.

By nature a student rather than a practitioner, he was deeply interested in the scientific investigation on which all medicine is based. Had life and health been granted him, his name might have stood high on the honor roll of those whose lives have been devoted to medical research; but this was not to be. While still in the early prime of manhood, his health began to fail; and after several years of suffering he died in 1889, at the age of forty-two.

The writer never knew Dr. Robinson personally, but she recalls vividly his striking aspect; the tall figure, stooping slightly, the keen, intellectual face, already marked with lines of suffering, the brilliant, sombre eyes.

"A man of mark," was one's first thought; one's second, "and of sorrows!" His friends recall him as "a quiet fellow"; mostly silent in company, but flashing out now and then some keen sword-thrust of wit. Those who knew him best loved him best.

So today, the two brothers come back together to the old town that reared them. The younger, in the full splendor of his powers, acclaimed as the foremost living poet of America, seems to lead the elder out of the shadow into a light partly reflected from his own; but only partly. Dean Robinson, too, was a seeker, a seer of visions.

"He knew more at twenty," says E.A.R., "than I shall ever know."

Now, through his brother's gift to the hospital, some of the visions may be realized. If as we believe, nothing good is lost, we may say with another poet mourning for his dead,

> "Somewhere, surely, afar,
> In the sounding labour-house vast
> Of being, is practised that strength,
> Zealous, beneficent, firm!"
>
> L.E.R.

SEPTEMBER 15, 1931 (MACKAYE)

1. Percy MacKaye's son, Robert Keith MacKaye.

NOVEMBER 4, 1931 (MRS. RIDGELY TORRENCE)

(From the London *Times*)

1. *Proust and Dickens.*

Sir,—I wonder whether those who have already been struck by the relation between Marcel Proust and Charles Dickens—whom, as is well known, he read with luminous enthusiasm and comprehension—have remembered a certain passage in "Dombey and Son"?

"He did not know why. For all that the child observed, and felt, and thought, that night—the present and the absent; what was then and what had been—were blended like the colours in the rainbow, or in the plumage of rich birds when the sun is shining on them, or in the softening sky when the same sun is setting. The many things he had had to think of lately, passed before him in the music; not as claiming his attention over again, or as likely ever more to occupy it, but as peacefully disposed of and gone. A solitary window, gazed through years ago, looked out upon an ocean, miles and miles away; upon its waters, fancies, busy with him only yesterday, were hushed and lulled to rest like broken waves. The same mysterious murmur he had wondered at, when lying on his couch upon the beach, he thought he still heard sounding through his sister's song, and through the hum of voices, and the tread of feet, and having some part in the faces flitting by, and even in the heavy gentleness of Mr. Toots, who frequently came up to shake him by the hand. Through the universal kindness he still thought he heard it, speaking to him; and even his old-fashioned reputation seemed to be allied to it, he knew not how."

Truly yours,
M. Ciolkowska.

Via del Babuino, 46, Rome.

AUGUST 31, 1932 (MRS. RICHARDS)

1. *Nicodemus.*

MARCH 3, 1933 (MRS. RICHARDS)

1. and 2. Both references are to detective stories, of which E. A. R. read an inordinate number, often two in a night. His only stipulation in regard to them, he said, was that they have no pretension to literary quality.

AUGUST 10, 1933 (ISAACS)

1. *Amaranth.*